Writing For Professionals
2nd Edition

Dr. Daryl D. Green

"When Daryl Green makes his case on the benefits of working with purpose and passion, he is not just spouting theory. He is sharing valuable, first-hand insight. The wise guidance in his books comes from a special place – straight from Daryl's own dynamic achievements as a classic self-starter in the world of self-publishing."

Caesar Andrews, the Paul A. Leonard Distinguished Visiting Chair in Ethics at the University of Nevada, Reno, and Author's Brother-in-Law

"Writing and publishing a book can be overwhelming, causing many talented writers to steer away from a lifelong dream. This book takes this overwhelming task and simplifies it. A must read for anyone who wants to be a published author."

Jalene Nemec, Author of *Great Customer Service*

"Dr. Green's book includes helpful information for novice writers: how to better understand and influence their readers, how to distinguish types of publishers, and how to work toward their goals of getting published."

Sarah Senter, M.S. Library and Information Sciences

"I am sure I was not the only student in Dr. Green's class who was terrified when he told the class each person would publish a book by the end of the semester. Dr. Green made it an easier process and guided the class step-by-step on how to publish a book. I am happy that he wrote this book."

**Alla Jacques, MBA
Career Services Specialist, ITT Technical Institute, Co-Author of *The Struggle to Become Young***

"Publications can be effectively leveraged as valuable professional capital. Dr. Green's book, Writing for Professionals, outlines practical guidelines for individuals looking to utilize publication as a tool for attaining both social and professional advancement."

Douglas E. Carrington Slaughter, MIT Alumnus and Emerging Leader

"Dr. Daryl Green has developed a blueprint for ambitious young professionals seeking to publish their expertise and advance their careers. His book offers key strategies for those wanting to break away from the expected. It is for those who want to soar."

Dr. Daniel Graves, Program Director, Management & Leadership, Lincoln Memorial University School of Business

2nd Edition

Technical edit by Amanda Shaffer

For information on ordering in bulk, please contact:

PMLA
P.O. Box 32733
Knoxville, TN 37930-2733
(865) 602-7858
advice@darylgreen.org

Table of Contents

Acknowledgment

I want to thank God for this awesome opportunity to help others gain a more fulfilled life. I do not take my success for granted. I realize that I did not arrive where I am today without assistance. I want to personally thank my wife, Estraletta, for her continued support. She is truly a virtuous and gifted lady. Additionally, I want to thank my children - Mario, Sharlita, and Demetrius. I want to thank my parents, the late Edward Elias and Annette Green Elias, and my mother-in-law, the late Mrs. Lucy Andrews, for providing me with such good advice about life. Lastly, I want to thank the many role models who have entered my life and helped shape my character. May God watch over you on this journey.

I also want to thank everyone who read, evaluated, and commented on my book, because your feedback was critical to my success. Finally, I want to thank the millions of readers who have read my columns, books, and articles. It is an honor to serve humanity in this special way. I will never stop searching for new opportunities to leave this world better than I found it.

Preface

My mother called one day, brimming with excitement. She was watching a popular court TV show, and the featured couple was having the kind of drama that drives television ratings. The husband had a book in his hand, and the judge asked him what he was reading. He replied, "*Awakening the Talents Within* by Daryl Green." Then, I went crazy too. Here was my name, and the name of my book, mentioned on national television. By writing that book, my name was called out to millions of people across the country. This unexpected publicity was due solely to my process of moving ideas, from concept to the reality of written word.

When my first book was published, suddenly newspapers wanted to quote me; talk shows wanted to interview me; my neighbors and friends wanted my autograph. However, I was still the same person. My book did not change my immediate job. In fact, some managers felt it was a distraction. My published credentials granted me a new expert status that augmented my influence in society. I experienced the elevation of the publishing platform.

I find that many professionals seek to increase their power at work and at home: yet, even those with inspired ideas may lack the qualifications to get their opinions heard. Gaining that influence is critical in achieving an elevated level of success. When an individual is recognized through a writing platform, people tend to accept their advice and recommendations. By publishing, I discovered the power of written word to transform my life and the lives of countless others.

As soon as I entered the workforce, I found a passion for assisting people in committing their ideas to publishable form. *Writing for Professionals: The Definitive Handbook for Gaining More Influence* provides individuals with authoritative writing tools. It offers strategies, practical guidelines, resources, and a host of suggestions to help with publishing goals.

The advice in this book can be useful for a wide variety of professions, including business executives, teachers, scientists, engineers, attorneys, and many others. It is geared toward professionals who desire to publish nonfiction in areas such as self-help, how-to, biography and management. By learning the art of writing, professionals have a practical way of gaining influence and becoming a powerful change agent in their communities.

1
Introduction

"If you dream of something worth doing and then simply go to work on it and don't think anything of personalities, or emotional conflicts, or of money, or of family distractions; it is amazing how quickly you get through those 5,000 steps."

**-Edwin Land,
American Scientist and Inventor**

Rapid development of communication technologies has enhanced globalization, making the world a vast land of opportunity. A professional in the 21st century is capable of influencing millions of people from thousands of cultures. Unfortunately, this land is only conquerable by those who understand how it works. One of the fastest ways to influence others is by sharing your expertise. Writing and publishing bring recognition to your name and acknowledgement of your abilities. Although fewer people may enjoy reading, America still appreciates good, quality content. This is evident in the popularity of eBook-compatible technologies, such as the iPhone or the Kindle. Gaining influence is critical in achieving any substantial success in life. When an individual has a platform as an established writer, people tend to listen. This effect allows the writer's opinion to be heard.

On a global scale, we are under severe economic pressures. Professionals must weigh their options as they balance a career with personal obligations. Giant organizations aim to streamline everything. They drop processes and people that are not intrinsic pieces of their bottom-line.

Some of us sit back and hope that business will create more jobs. With a weak economic growth rate of 3%, these jobs will not appear anytime soon. This is a dire forecast for the 15 million unemployed Americans. Clever individuals will begin to develop their own career strategies. The goal is to stay afloat in an uncertain future.

Writing for Professionals provides critical tools for establishing clout through the writing medium. This book is designed for a variety of individuals, from the novice to the most seasoned professional. We will focus on non-fiction writing in areas such as self-help, how-to, biography, management, business, and other informative writing styles. Consulting experts Eldridge Elsom, Jr. and Mark Eldridge explain, "A book published in your name enhances your business reputation. It does not matter what field you are in or how you have approached marketing in the past."[1] Any reader with a deeper aspiration to impress can benefit from this information.

This book will assist business owners, ministers, entrepreneurs, lecturers, consultants, educators, professional speakers, trainers, politicians, authors, or anyone else who desires to share information.

---

[1] *The Obvious Expert* by Elsom, Jr. & Mark Eldridge

Writing non-fiction can be a catalyst for achieving your greatest publishing ambitions (See Figure 1).

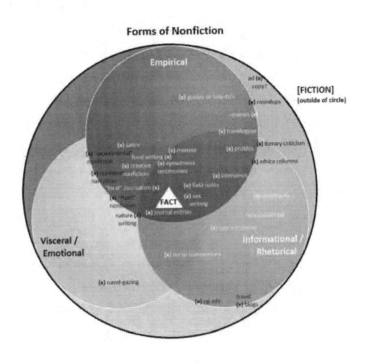

Source and Credit: David Miller, Author of *16 Non-Fiction Forms and How to Write Them*

Being a published author can help a professional in many ways, including promotions, status, monetary rewards, speaking engagements, and new business prospects. You will witness an instant boost to your credibility. Elizabeth Foote-Smith, author of *Opportunities in Writing Careers,* explains the unlimited opportunities in writing: "With today's technology, you need the ability to express yourself using written words. Business is no longer based on face to face interactions. To survive in this world, you need to be a capable writer."[2] Those who understand this reality always rise above their competition. Strategic writing is a key to unlock many new opportunities. Effective writing can mean new financial gain, such as a paid magazine column.

Getting published is not an easy road. People must carry passion for what they are doing. Society has plenty of "would-be superstars" who couldn't finish what they started. A professional needs to identify the market – who will want to pay for the product? After finishing this book, readers will have a proven blueprint for successfully getting published. This could lead to significant influence in the corporate environment, as well as local, national, and global communities.

---

[2] *Opportunities in Writing Careers* by Elizabeth Foote-Smith

"You got a chance to do the best you can."

**—Deacon Willie Coleman Robinson,
Father of University of Tennessee Basketball
Player Larry Robinson**

PART I – BACKGROUND

2
Power & Influence

"Self-starters dream. They're imaginative and creative, too. But they are also go-getters: independent individuals ready to turn their dreams into reality. They're willing to take risks and are not afraid to blaze their own trails."

**- Blythe Camenson,
Author of *Careers for Self-Starters***

Cindy's study group gathers around to address the instructor's exercise. It isn't a difficult project: a typical management problem she has been familiar with for over 20 years. Yet, Cindy's group ignores her input in lieu of Laura, a charismatic business assistant. Every time Laura makes a suggestion, the group agrees with her while Cindy finds herself defending her position. When the instructor asks for group presentations, it is Laura that presents, not Cindy. Cindy's group addresses the problem incorrectly. Retrospectively, Cindy fails to understand why her group doesn't listen to her.

Today, many managers operate like dominant gorillas in charge of their families. People in organizations generally follow the person in power, not necessarily the best thinkers. This is called the Alpha Principle. Harry Beckwith, marketing author, states that most organizations operate like apes. He notes, "The alphas dictate what the group does and thinks. But are alphas the best decision-makers? Not necessarily. Alphas are just better at getting and keeping power." Poorly-skilled managers cause a lot of unnecessary stress to employees because they don't understand how to treat people. Employees then bring this stress home to their families, thereby creating more problems. In today's hypercompetitive and political environment, most professionals need to leverage power within the organization to get things accomplished. Therefore, understanding how power operates in business is vital for success.

There are a variety of ways individuals can obtain influence in contemporary organizations. Skip Press, author of *How to Write What You Want & Sell What You Write*, talks about the edge that providing meaningful content means in society: "Truly great writers create works that have a lasting, beneficial effect on generations of readers, often helping to bring about a change of understanding and social custom in their own society."[3] Taking on this type of leadership involves a combination of power and influence. Leadership can be defined as the ability to inspire, guide, and direct others. Leaders get people to do things they wouldn't normally do alone. Power is a key component of leadership. Power is the ability of a person to steer others toward a desired goal. In most companies, power is often misunderstood as a right to dominate others. Given this dynamic of business operations, managers need to understand their organizations. James Gibson, John Ivancevich, James Donelly, Jr., and Robert Konopaske, authors of *Organizations*, argue that individuals need to understand how larger groups operate.[4]

---

[3] *How to Write What You Want & Sell What You Write* by Skip Press

[4] *Organizations* by James Gibson, John Ivancevich, James Donelly, Jr., and Robert Konopaske

In many organizations, there is a power struggle. Five interpersonal bases of power are summarized: legitimate power, reward power, coercive power, referent power, and expert power. In legitimate power, a person's ability to influence others is given by being in a position of power. The person's influence is authorized solely by his title in the organization. There is little an individual in this type of group can achieve if he or she does not possess legitimate power.

Coercive and reward power are based on the same premise as legitimate power. It is a person's ability to reward or punish the behavior of others.[5] In fact, these sources of power are often used to support legitimate power. If the person is not in a position to apply coercive or reward power, gaining influence may prove difficult. The above items are considered organizational power.

When individuals do not have a definitive title, they should be strategic in garnering esteem within their group. The two major factors in these organizations are referent and expert power.

---

[5] *Organizations* by James Gibson, John Ivancevich, James Donelly, Jr., and Robert Konopaske

Referent power is based on a person's charisma, due to his personality or style of behavior. Gibson, Ivancevich, Donelly, and Konopaske maintain that the strength of a person's charisma correlates directly with the strength of the person's referent power.[6] This power can be effective in leading others to make better decisions. People will listen to the person because they instinctively trust confident leadership abilities. Unfortunately, not everyone has this type of magnetic personality.

Finally, expert power is the ability to influence others based on distinctive expertise. Even when an individual may have a low rank in an organization, expert power makes the person invaluable. Expert power can relate to administrative or technical knowledge, or to other personal attributes. Expert power speaks to the Law of Scarcity. The more difficult a person is to replace, the greater the individual's expert power is within the organization.

Individuals can gain expert power in several ways. First, a person can learn about the organization's specific needs or deficiencies.

---

[6] *Organizations* by James Gibson, John Ivancevich, James Donelly, Jr., and Robert Konopaske

The person will then seek to fill this knowledge gap. For example, a small consulting firm may lack sufficient promotional skills. An employee with marketing abilities could provide this additional service to the organization. Thus, the employee gains power. Employees can also take additional training and obtain special certifications geared toward the needs of their company.

Alternatively, individuals can become an authority in a particular area to become a "hot commodity." Furthermore, a person who trains, lectures, teaches, and writes about his or her area of expertise establishes clout both inside and outside the organization. Expert power may not propel an individual into the next manager level. However, it will offer great influence in the organization as well as the community. Influence becomes mobile and makes the person a "hot commodity" in the marketplace.

WRITING FACTS

Elance.com

Busy professionals can look to Elance.com for writing assistance. Elance.com, a freelance website, allows customers to solicit work from a variety of outsourcing services which include programmers, designers, office support, translators, marketers, researchers, and many other disciplines. Potential employers see a website that attracts over 500,000 talented freelancers. For the freelancer, there is an opportunity to bid on 48,000 jobs, worth $480K.[7] Below is an analysis of Elance.com's marketing mix:

Service – Elance.com allows businesses to post a job opening to freelancers at potential savings.

Placement – All transactions occur on the website.

Price - The company charges a $10 fee to each business to post a job. Elance.com also takes a small portion of what gets paid to contractors. It is considered low-to-medium costs.

Promotions – Much of the effort appears to be publicity and word-of-mouth referrals.

Elance.com allows a business to post a job and invites freelance workers possessing the requisite skills to make a bid. The company charges a $10 fee to each business to post a job and takes a small portion of what gets paid to contractors.[8] For potential employers, Elance.com provides ratings, previous feedback, and tests to evaluate each contractor's ability. For freelancers and contractors, it offers real-time feedback. When Elance.com gets repeat business or new business, this is a worthy indication of superior services.

In summary, individuals accomplish greater feats in groups where they have power and influence. Any effective professional needs to understand how to gain this level of esteem. As businesses fight to stay alive in a tough economy, there is an increasing need for effective leaders.

---

[7] Elance.com

[8] Joshkotsay.com

Acquiring influence becomes a premium for emerging leaders.

In this discussion, we have demonstrated that most organizations have a variety of power types. Some managers fear losing their power and are unwilling to share decision-making processes. This is unfortunate because entrusting competent employees to make better decisions is a catalyst for high-performance teams. Insightful professionals must understand the best ways to influence others. Individuals do not have to be the boss to obtain certain types of power within an organization.

"Successful planning takes time, as well as management of that irreplaceable resource."

- Erik Sherman

3
Non-Fiction Writing

"Everyone wants to be outstanding, but no one wants to stand-out."

**- Rev. Richard Brown, Jr.,
Senior Pastor of Payne Avenue Missionary
Baptist Church**

Effective writing is a dynamic way of influencing others. Without an authoritative voice, readers will not take the message seriously. There are a variety of writing styles best suited for providing more influence at work, home, and abroad.

Non-fiction writing focuses on factual content, intended primarily for informational purposes instead of entertainment. Some details in non-fiction writing may contain aspects of opinion, but the writing should focus on concrete facts for credibility.[9] Therefore, the distinction between fiction and non-fiction pertains to intent. Some non-fiction characteristics include:

- Real people, events, places, and ideas

- Non-fiction is narrated by a real person

- Presentation of facts, true-life experiences, or discussion of ideas

- Non-fiction is written for a specific audience

- Author's attitude toward the subject or reader is displayed through the word choice and writing style[10]

---

[9] *Definition of Non-Fiction Writing* by eHow.com

[10] *Non-Fiction Writing* by Misshannigan.com

In the past, many people associated non-fiction writing with journalism and freelance writing. They were the language experts who provided their knowledge in a variety of writing mediums.[11] This is no longer the case as many professionals use non-fiction writing on a daily basis. When a doctor writes a letter to an editor about a health matter, the doctor is employing non-fiction writing.

Non-fiction writing is broken into four basic categories: narrative writing, expository writing, persuasive writing, and descriptive writing. Narrative writing tells a real-life story about a person, event, or place.[12] Examples of narrative writing include essays, journals, autobiographies, and memoirs. Expository writing informs readers on a chosen topic. Examples of expository writing include business letters, research reports, and book proposals.

In persuasive writing, the author presents reasons to act or think in a certain fashion. He or she establishes a position on a divided issue and then argues for his or her side.

---

[11] *10 Types of Non-Fiction Freelance Writing* by Freelancesprout.com

[12] *The Four Types of Non-Fiction Explained* by Eliteediting.com

Editorials are a common example of persuasive writing. Lastly, descriptive writing creates mental images for readers using figurative language meant to stimulate all five senses. Descriptive writing may include essays, memoirs, and critiques of any kind. Table 1 shows an assortment of non-fiction writing genres.

Expository	Persuasive	Narrative	Descriptive
• Almanac	• Editorial	• Creative Non-Fiction	• Book Review
• Article	• eZine	• Column	• Business Letters
• Autobiography	• Journalism	• Diary/Journal	• Consultant Report
• Biography	• Letter to the Editor	• Essay	• Design Document
• Blog	• Media Release	• Travel Log	• Diagram
• Blueprint	• Newsletter	• Twitter Updates	• Dictionary
• Book			• Encyclopedia
• Book Proposal			• How-To/Instructional
• Brochure			• Literary Criticism
• eBook			• Memoir
• Query Letter			
• Speech			
• Statute			
• Web Content			

Many people are reluctant to share their ideas in writing. However, insightful professionals understand the power of written words. David Miller, who is the senior editor of Matador and BETA magazine, reaffirms the importance of non-fiction writing: "Non-fiction describes communicative work…an interesting way to delineate non-fiction forms is to look at them in terms of how accurately they reflect the writer's experience, beliefs, and emotions in real life…[13]" Individuals need to write for greater clarity if they want to be successful. Effective writing is concise, clear, and original. As with every other skill, individuals will need to practice for higher writing success.

Take your writing seriously. It is a powerful method of communication. Demonstrate your commitment by conducting thorough research, developing a level of expertise, and writing with passion. You will need to utilize adept writing mechanics to get the job done (See Figure 2).

---

[13] *16 Non-Fiction Forms and How to Write Them* by David Miller

Figure 2. Effective Writing Matrix

- Be concise and clear.

- Write with your reader in mind.

- Prepare for book skimming or scanning.

- Create relevant information.

- Construct simple, well-written information.

- Be well organized and logical.

- Use effective grammar and style.

Persuasive writing need not be complicated. The process can be broken down into several basic steps. The first step is to schedule time for your writing. There is no special rule; some people write in short sprints, while others take a marathon approach. This can take weeks, months, or over a year. Find a time frame that works for you.

Second, you need to set a deadline for the completion of your project. Many people procrastinate when writing a book. A person should not begin this writing journey until he or she is fully committed. One trick I have taught clients is to imagine there is a class assignment of writing a 50 page essay. Remember having to do a research paper in high school? It's the same principle. Set your sights on the deadline and get it done.

Another critical step for novice writers is to review authors you may admire, but to develop your own style. You are special, and you want your writing to be unique. Let readers discover your personal expertise through your writing style. With the emergence of the Internet, an individual can hire a writing doctor to polish his or her writing.

However, you can't hire passion or flair. Professionals should identify what makes their work unique, but they should not lose sight of their reasons for writing. Jay Levinson, Rick Frishman, and Michael Larson, authors of *Guerrilla Marketing for Writers*, note: "The information an author shares in a non-fiction book is more important than how the book is written."[14] A professional author who keeps the reader in mind will quickly advance toward his or her publishing objectives (See Figure 3).

---

[14] *Guerrila Marketing for Writers* by Levinson, Jay, Rick Frishman, and Michael Larsen

Figure 3. The Various Types of Non-Fiction Writing for Professionals

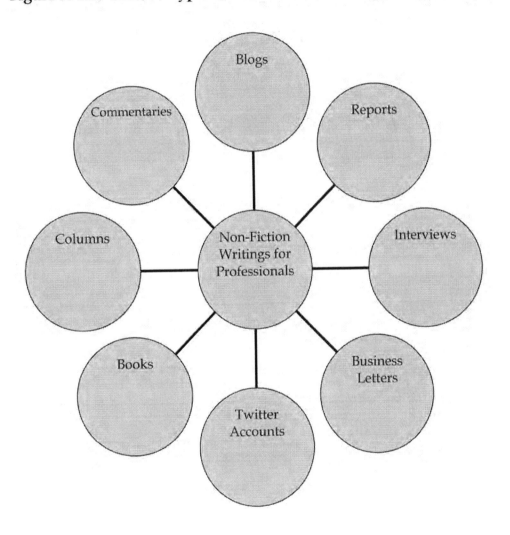

"...it is not enough to be an expert, know you are an expert, and announce to the world that you are an expert. Recognition comes only when you take the necessary actions to position yourself as a premier and obvious expert."

**- Eldridge Elsom, Jr. & Mark Eldridge,
Author of *The Obvious Expert***

4
Value Creation

"You will always encounter folk who don't agree with what you want to do....Always hope for help, but expect the contrary. It is the entrepreneur's dilemma."

- Dr. Bruce Winston,
Author of *Be a Leader for God's Sake*

If an individual can solve another person's problems, he or she will earn a friend and generate value. This newfound worth allows for greater influence in relevant circles. Today's organizations strategically attempt to generate value for their customers. Writing provides an excellent avenue for proving worth in expert fields.

Individuals who want to create maximum value need to aim their writing at providing useful solutions to common problems. Through editorials and commentaries, professionals can share personal experiences, inspiration, and strong opinions that call communities to action. Certain websites can help achieve this objective as well. Through word-of-mouth, I heard about a website called Elance.com for freelancers and entrepreneurs. Elance.com allows individuals and organizations to bid out quality work for the best price.

On Elance.com, I was amazed at the different people bidding from around the world. Conventional wisdom suggests that someone bidding for work in India at $5.00 per hour versus a bid from someone New York at $60.00 per hour would be an obvious decision.

However, I have purchased services from Elance.com where the price was not the prime consideration. I evaluated the individual's experience and identified what it was worth for me to get it done. I was ultimately aiming for the best value. Likewise, professionals need to arm themselves with skills to generate personal merit in relationship to globalization.

For many people, the concept of value is vague. An exact definition of value depends on the individual, but it could be defined as the net bundle of benefits the customer derives from a product or service. Mark Johnston and Greg Marshall, authors of *Relationship Selling*, argue that an individual must understand the customer to establish value.[15] Furthermore, Paul Peter and James Donnelly, authors of *Marketing Management*, argue that the starting point in the buying process is the consumer's recognition of an unsatisfied need. The customer must remain the focus for any sustainable business success.

Value creation must be a strategic and deliberate concept for professionals. Mark Johnston and Greg Marshall maintain that perceived value is in the eyes of the customer. Therefore, perceived value will vary.

A professional's biggest challenge is in selling this value with consistency. Being strategic about these business relationships is not simple. Organizations must clearly understand the external motivation within their market in order to create lasting customer value. The external environment is considered anything outside of the organization's control. External environment factors include economic stability, legal-political shifts, technological growth, social-cultural norms, and natural changes.

Businesses can't hide from the impacts of globalization. According to Dr. James Canton's *The Extreme Future*, there will be a global war for "Smart Talent."[16] In fact, it will be the cornerstone of competitive advantage. The most educated, skilled, and experienced employees will be in high demand.

Worldwide competition and shortage of workers makes diversity a center-point for international businesses. Globalization forces many corporations to re-think their approaches.

Thomas Friedman, author of *The World is Flat*, notes the progression of globalization. Globalization 1.0 (started in 1492 when Columbus set sail and

---

[15] *Relationship Selling* by Mark Johnston and Greg Marshall
[16] *The Extreme Future* by Dr. James Canton

lasted until about 1800) was driven by the dynamic force of global integration between countries.[17] Globalization 2.0 (roughly 1800 to 2000) was driven by global integration between multinational companies. In Globalization 3.0, the force is being driven by the power of individuals to collaborate and compete globally. This level of globalization benefits from a diverse field of constituents. Understanding how to generate perceived consumer worth on a global scale will be vital for sustaining business success.

Twenty-first-century organizations can no longer implement value creation in a vacuum. Ken Favaro, author of *Put Value Creation First*, further suggests that placing a priority on value creation gives businesses two advantages over their competition: the first is capital and the second is talent. Favaro argued that successful value creators never suffer from capital shortage.[18]

Value focuses on the relationship between the customer's expectations

---

[17] *The World is Flat* by Thomas L. Friedman

[18] *Put Value Creation First* by Ken Favaro

of a product or service and the amount paid for it. C.K. Prahalad and Vemkatram Ramaswamy, authors of *The Future of Competition*, further reasoned that twenty-first-century corporations must adapt their value creation system to fit the global scale. They noted the new system is an individual-centered, co-creation of worth between consumers and organizations.[19] Few executives take the time to explain their values, but this will be increasingly important if companies hope to expand success in their global market.

With 15 million people unemployed in America, it's important for professionals to build a niche. There are plenty of experienced professors, doctors, lawyers, school teachers, and others in the unemployed ranks. Therefore, creating a unique set of skills is a matter of necessity. Future employers are potential customers.

Creating value for them will unlock employment opportunities. Dr. Lynda Falkenstein, a niche market expert, put it this way, "Understanding your customer's perceptions of the world is an absolute must for one major

---

[19] *The Future of Competition* by C.K. Prahalad and Vemkatram Ramaswamy

reason; that is, no one buys something just because you want to sell it."[20] In order to be effective, professionals should address the consumer's problems for creating lasting value.

---

[20] *Nichecraft* by Lynda Falkenstein

"More writers are rejected by the big houses than are accepted...The most difficult challenge for any author today is not getting published. It's deciding what publishing option to choose and then figuring out how to get noticed."

- M.J. Rose and Angela Adair-Hoy,
Authors of *How to Publish and Promote Online*

PART II – CRITICAL STEPS

5
Author Platform: Building Social Networks

"Any fool can criticize, condemn, and complain—and most fools do. But it takes character and self-control to be understanding and forgiving."

- Dale Carnegie, Author of
How to Win Friends and Influence People

Without a good platform for launching their writing, professionals will find themselves in difficult situations. However, there are numerous writing mediums to consider. When Alaska's Governor Sarah Palin announced she was resigning abruptly in July 2009, many people thought she was history.[21] Those individuals did not understand the value of an author's platform. Through the use of Twitter and other social media accounts, Palin understood how to leverage power through a variety of communication mediums. She quickly secured a book deal with HarperCollins to produce her memoirs.

Palin knew she had plenty of options to raise her visibility. In 1996, Palin was the mayor of Wasila, Alaska at the age of 32 years old. She made $64,000 a year. In 2012 at the age of 48, Palin writes her opinions in columns, speaks to large crowds, and provides commentary as a Fox News Analyst.[22] Her author platform provides over $1 million a year. For many high-profile individuals, the public speaking circuit offers a lucrative living and a significant platform.

---

[21] *Options Abound for Palin After Alaska Governorship* by Foxnews.com

[22] *Salary* by Parade (Sunday, April 15, 2012)

What *exactly* is an author platform? An author's platform is the medium that brings the author to life for readers.[23] Developing the proper stage may require a person to move beyond his or her comfort zone. Experts Barbara Gaughen and Ernest Weckbaugh maintain, "The obligation to meet the public, either one-on-one, in front of hundreds, or facing a TV camera broadcasted to millions is an essential part of promotion."[24] Some authors' platforms include writing blogs or columns, participating in speaking venues, interacting as a radio talk show host or guest, or being a key authority figure in accredited organizations. A large following can produce incredible results, such as obtaining a highly profitable contract with a major publisher.

Another critical result of having an author's platform is generating influence within the professional environment. Therefore, creating the right type of author platform is important. No author or speaker is completely created in the same ways. Individuals need to develop a platform that best fits their personality and style. This does require many people to exit their

---

[23] *Get Published* by Susan Driscoll & Diane Gedymin

comfort zone. For example, a reserved professional may eventually need to lecture in front of a large audience. Shy individuals should consider social networking as part of their core promotional strategy.

In today's hectic environment, instantaneous Internet access has laid a new foundation in relating to the target market. Given this revelation, social networking offers an effective solution for nearly every professional. Social networking allows individuals and organizations to cater certain marketing campaigns to specific groups. With more than 900 million users, Facebook has become the juggernaut of social networking. Professionals can use Facebook as an avenue for relationship building.[25] Steven Holzner, author of *Facebook Marketing*, argues that social networking is not the same as other conventional methods: "...traditional marketing methods won't work here. In Facebook, the users are in charge, not the marketers, and that's a fact we have to live with." Holzner maintains that users must understand the new rules of social marketing. The greatest influence is only established with the

---

[24]*Book Blitz* by Barbara Gaughen & Ernest Weckbaugh

[25] *Facebook Marketing* by Steven Holzner

right kind of author's platform.

"Control is number one on the list of reasons to publish independently."

**– Jerrold Jenkins and Ann Stanton,
Authors of *Publish to Win***

6
Book Publication & Other Writing Outlets

"By and large, there is no such thing as 'something for nothing.' In the long run you get exactly that for which you pay, whether you are buying an automobile or a loaf of bread."

- Napoleon Hill

If I were to choose one writing medium for gaining the most influence, I would select a book. I have been blessed to publish in a variety of mediums, paid and unpaid. I enjoy writing on contemporary issues impacting businesses, societies, and global communities.

Over 3,000 online publishers and content providers have used my articles around the world. My first syndicated column *Family Vision*, done through the Newspaper Publishers Association, reached over 200 newspapers with more than 15 million readers across America. I have also been a freelance writer and guest columnist for various publications, including *Knoxville News Sentinel*, *Knoxville Enlightener*, *Kingdom Business Magazine*, *Discovery Christian Magazine*, *New-Wave Christian Magazine*, and the *American Journal of Biblical Theology*. With all this stated, publishing several books has been the most life-changing experience for my professional career. All of my writing opportunities sprouted from my first book, *My Cup Runneth Over*, in 1998.

Some might call me nostalgic about my book preference. However, society still places a high value on literacy, even if it is just talk. Regardless of the writing medium, individuals need to take these activities seriously. Proper planning is integral to becoming a successfully published author. There are a variety of publishing options, but this chapter focuses on effectively publishing a book.

It may seem obvious, but if you want to be published, you need to understand the publishing industry. Surprisingly enough, many otherwise serious writers do not take time to do their homework. With the emergence of new publishing technologies and easy access to a global platform via the Internet, the publishing world is in a state of constant change. The major purpose for traditional publishers is to turn a profit. Therefore, they look for broad subject books with mass appeal. They normally launch twenty or more books at the same time with the hope of one hitting it big. Mergers of the major publishers, the advent of large booksellers such as Barnes & Noble or Amazon.com, and niche marketing of small, independent publishers continue to reshape the industry standards. There are over 60,000 books published every year. Over 53% of these books are purchased outside of traditional bookstores.

Today's major publishers include Random House or Bantam, Doubleday, Dell, Simon & Schuster, Penguin, Putnam, and HarperCollins. [26] For the most part, these large publishers are concentrated in the east, primarily around New York. The traditional path to publishing has been to write a manuscript or book, locate a literary agent or salesperson, find the right publisher, submit the manuscript for review, receive an offer from the publisher, and finally get published and paid.

Times have changed. The major publishers continue to lose money. They can't afford to risk publishing an unknown writer. Therefore, large publishing houses now prefer to publish previously established writers, celebrities, marquee names, and any other authors with a significant following. Publishing companies operate as businesses, and they can't afford to groom new writers. The modern publishing model for larger houses monitors the small publishers and self-publishers until an author achieves a high level of success. The large publishing company will then request the author to sign them for a book deal. This reduces the risk for the big publishing groups and allows them to get a seasoned package.

---

[26] *Jump Start Your Book Sales* by Marilyn & Tom Ross

New writers and midlist authors, who are not yet established and less marketable, are forced to publish elsewhere. Publishing gurus Tom and Marilyn Ross suggest that many large publishers are only looking for the big names.[27] Tom and Marilyn explain, "Today, the attitude of New York publishers is that they only want household names or sure-fire books." This fact works against the emerging or midlist author. The good news is that opportunities abound. The vast majority of books are not published by the major publishers. University presses, small publishers, and self-publishers are becoming the dominant forces in the literary market because they usually operate on non-traditional models. This often brings innovation and creativity to a stagnant industry. In general, authors can expect to be published in one of the following options:

- *Major Publisher/Commercial House* – These organizations are responsible for the complete publishing process, including editing, promotion, printing, and distribution. They generally receive over 15,000 unsolicited manuscripts to review per year, of which they tend to

---

[27] *Jump Start Your Book Sales* by Marilyn & Tom Ross

publish 200 or more.[28] Securing a literary agent is the most important step to acquire a book contract with a major publisher. The agent will provide payments to the author in the form of royalties that typically range from 5% to 15%.[29] The process is filled with a lot of waiting and uncertainty, but the payoff can be great.

- *Small Publisher/Independent Press* – These companies have responsibilities similar to those of a major publisher, but on a smaller scale. They generally publish fewer than 10 books per year. Most small publishers do not require an agent and are more receptive to new writers. [30] Due to their limited budgets, small publishers do not have the same exposure as larger publishers.

- *Vanity Press* – These businesses are rightfully considered the black sheep of the publishing industry and associated with business scams.

---

[28] *Publish to Win* by Jerrold Jenkins & Anne Stanton

[29] *Get Published* by Susan Driscoll & Diane Gedymin

[30] *Publish to Win* by Jerrold Jenkins & Anne Stanton

Vanity press is also called subsidized publishing. To the novice observer, vanity press may appear to be the same as self-publishing. It is not. In a vanity press, writers pay to be published. While self-publishing is designed for the author's advantage, vanity presses are designed for the company's own financial benefit. Stay away from vanity presses.

- _University Press_ – These groups represent a very unique publishing niche. They are non-profit organizations that publish books for the literary, social, and scholarly contribution. In most cases, the author does not need a literary agent. The royalties may be lower than with a traditional publisher, but the name recognition through a university press is worth consideration.

- _Self-Publishing_ – This publishing sector represents the mavericks, innovators, risk-takers, and entrepreneurs. The self-publisher takes on all of the responsibilities of the publishing process, thereby assuming all of the risks and rewards. When done effectively, the profit obtained from self-publishing far exceeds the traditional royalties of 5% to 15%. Many of the publishing functions can now be outsourced or contracted at the lowest price.

- *Publishing Portal* – This method provides a hybrid type of publishing. Some may consider them vanity presses because they will publish anyone, and they primarily make their money through authors buying their books. However, publishing portals heavily depend on technologies such as print-on-demand, which are profitable for writers. With their ease of acceptance and convenience for writers, publishing portals continue to instigate change within traditional publishing.

Professionals can enjoy a variety of publishing mediums. This exhaustive list of publishing options outlines plenty of alternatives for getting a book into print. The critical factor is to identify the best medium for the right purpose.

In any business venture, building a great product is important. Publishing a book is no different. If you want to get noticed, you will need a great title, an appealing book cover, and flawless writing with a unique style. In creating the right strategy, the professional should consider several variables including the product or book, the product placement or distribution channel, the price, promotional ventures, and methods to measure results.

As the first and possibly most important step, a book must be developed that is of high quality and captures the attention of its targeted audience. Jerrold Jenkins and Anne Stanton, authors of *Publish to Win*, suggest that the initial phase must start with a good idea. They explain, "When authors create a non-fiction or how-to book, they are providing information for the reader. They are imparting knowledge, research, instruction, data, facts, assistance, advice, intelligence, or wisdom." An author must also understand how people are influenced in order to connect with his or her audience. Dale Carnegie first published *How to Win Friends and Influence People* in 1937.[31] Today, this classic has remained a staple as a personal performance tool for millions.

---

[31] *How to Win Friends and Influence People* by Dale Carnegie

A countless number of sales people have sharply increased their success rates by using his principles. Many people of other professions have achieved these optimal results as well. Carnegie felt that instead of condemning individuals, the focus of one's effort should be on trying to understand them. To influence an individual, a person must understand why they do what they do.

A second and critical step is that customers need easy access to your book. This placement is related to the distribution channel. Professionals must decide where customers are most likely to purchase the book. Is it at a retail store, a seminar, direct mail, or on the Internet? Dan Poynter, the Godfather of Self-Publishing, explains, "The secret of effective book distribution is to make the title available in places with a high concentration of potential buyers."[32] Potential buyers are simply the target audience of the book. In self-publishing, an individual maximizes his time by only focusing on where potential readers will likely purchase the book.

As a third step, professionals must decide on the right price for the

---

[32] *The Self-Publishing Manual* by Dan Poynter

book. What are readers willing to pay for your book as compared to other similar books currently on the market? Jenkins and Stanton argue, "Conventional wisdom suggests that, as an independent publisher, you can earn up to 50 percent of a book's cover price compared to the much smaller fraction collected as royalties." It is imperative that individuals carefully develop a pricing strategy by analyzing the pricing of related books in the market.

Promoting the book is a fourth and vital step to any successful publishing project. If buyers are unaware of the book, they are unable to purchase it. Promotions include publicity and advertising. Publicity is considered free promotion, but individuals have little control over how the message will be processed. Some publicity examples include articles, TV interviews, radio interviews, author websites, Facebook, Twitter, or social networks, and other free outlets. In advertising, professionals have the most control of their message. However, this medium is more expensive. Some advertising strategies include Google AdWords, radio announcements, infomercials, and other paid platforms.

A final and critical problem for most emerging authors is the lack of measuring tools that can help a writer understand if he is successful. The entrepreneurial approach, suggested in this book, is built on the author's ability to measure results and determine outcomes. Remember to measure results against your personal objectives for publishing. Only professionals who understand their target audience, show genuine concern for their audience, and focus on ways to help with obstacles inhibiting the audience's goals will gain the desired esteem. The more valuable the information, the more influence the author gains. This concept grows exponentially. Below are the publishing steps to follow:

1. Determine Writing Objectives

A professional must first establish his or her publishing objectives. What do you hope to accomplish in publishing this book? Do you hope to acquire influence, expertise, or wealth? It's important to answer this question upfront.

2. Establish Desired Outcomes

It is critical to determine what you expect as a result of publishing a book. If you do not know what success looks like, how can you expect to be successful? Many writers enter the publishing world with zero expectations. They hope that it will work out. However, entrepreneur publishing requires more thought. It will help determine your approach for publishing and what level of effort you need to apply.

3. Conduct Review of Related Writings

Review similar books in your subject area. Take it a step further and research your genre for ways to make your book stand-out.[33] Analyze the writing style and approach of other authors to develop your own.

4. Set Deadline for Publication

Some "would-be" authors have great intentions, but they never fulfill the dream of being published. One common problem is failure to set a publishing deadline and meet it. Determine a realistic date for completion. Write it down and stick with it.

---

[33] *How to Self-Publish & Market Your Book* by Mack & Sara Smith

5. Develop a Concept Aimed at a Problem

Most novice authors write a book for themselves. Consider writing a book to solve a problem for others or a problem within an industry. People will never stop looking for solutions to their problems.

6. Develop Promotional Strategy

Many writers fail without a good plan. Publishing a book is similar to running a business, and effective business people use a plan for implementing their business. Consider how you can best launch your book to your target readers. Identify your marketing strategy as it relates to your product, promotion, book distribution, and product price.

7. Select Preferred Publishing Medium

Authors must determine their preferred publishing method. The twenty-first century has provided an array of different publishing avenues. Many authors prefer the outright control of the self-publishing approach. Start your own publishing company (See Appendix B). If this is not possible, use a publishing portal with a great reputation and an established distribution channel.

8. Track Book Results and Compare with Desired Outcome

Once your work is published, continue to track the results against your desired outcome. Did you accomplish your goals? This is an ongoing process, so continue to measure your results.

9. Get Feedback from Target Audience

Renowned authors continue to get better. Likewise, one of your goals should be to always improve. Seek feedback from your readers when possible. It will help advance the quality of your books.

"Everything important to making or breaking a book happens before *the publication date."*

– Richard O'Connor,
Author of ***How to Market You & Your Book***

7
Conclusion

"It's been said that no one really motivates anyone else; all you can do is instill a positive attitude and hope it catches on."

**- Eddie Robinson,
Winningest College Football Coach**

In the 1939 movie classic *The Wizard of Oz*, a cyclone sweeps Dorothy Gale and her little dog Toto to the magical land of Oz. Dorothy wanders through the land, meeting some strange characters. There is the Scarecrow who desires a brain; the Tin Man who wants a heart; and the Cowardly Lion who hopes for courage. As Dorothy vows to help with each of their individual problems, she gains power and influence that speaks to the concept of indispensability.

The future is filled with uncertainty. More and more American jobs are outsourced every day. Companies continue to shrink in size, in hopes of being more competitive. Business executives understand the power of technology and subcontracting cheap labor to gain a business edge. Many workers rely on the mercy of their employers to stay gainfully employed. Sadly, many Americans do not fully understand the merits of indispensability in their lives. *Bloomberg Businessweek* magazine editor Josh Tyrangiel called indispensability the "new word of 2011." Tyrangiel notes, "How do we make people smarter and save them time?"

For my clients and students, I have emphasized the importance of building customer value in everything that they do. It is an attractive quality for personal branding strategy to be unforgettable. However, many workers operate in the dark shadows of their companies. Renowned preacher Richard S. Brown, Jr. proclaims to his audience, "Everyone wants to be outstanding, but no one wants to stand-out."

Yet, it is the standing-out that catches everyone's attention. I've written several books on this twenty-first-century theme, including *Breaking Organizational Ties*, *Publishing for Professionals*, and *Job Strategies for the 21st Century*. If you do the same things that you have always been doing, then you should not be surprised if you get the same results. Gaining influence is critical in achieving any substantial level of success in life. When an individual has a clear platform as an expert, people tend to listen. A person can often gain more influence in the office and the community with a clear personal strategy. This book has provided readers with a proven method for becoming indispensable in their organizations to build sustainability for their career.

Indispensability means adding value to your customers and organization. In the classic sense, indispensability means being absolutely essential or necessary. Yet, it goes to the heart of being relevant. Kivi Miller, author of *The Nonprofit Marketing Guide*, argues the importance of listening to your customers: "Every day presents an opportunity to learn more about the people you are trying to help and the people who are trying to help you."

Getting to know your target audience is critical. Are you indispensible to your organization or community? If not, then why not? Being indispensable is an attribute needed for individuals who want to compete in the twenty-first-century global environment. Everyone wants to feel needed. The concept of indispensability and being needed relates directly to gaining more influence in life. Legendary speaker Dale Carnegie understood the influential attributes of indispensability: "You can make more friends in two months by becoming interested in other people than you can in two years by trying to get other people interested in you." Therefore, an individual must be willing to understand the needs of others if he or she hopes to gain influence capable of sustaining his or her career goals.

With millions of people searching for full-time employment, it pays to stand-out among the crowd by building a unique set of indispensable skills. Twenty-first-century professionals need to re-develop their understanding of invaluable talent before it is too late.

References

Allen, Moira. *The Writer's Guide to Queries, Pitches & Proposal*. New York: Allworth Press 2001.

Allen, Moira. *Writing.com*. New York: Allworth Press 1999.

Brewer, Robert & Joanna Masterson. *Writer's Market*. Cincinnati, OH: Writer's Digest Books 2007.

Burgett, Gordon. *Publishing to Niche Markets*. Santa Maria, CA: Communication Unlimited 1995.

Carnegie, Dale. *How to Win Friends and Influence*. United States of America: Pocket 1998.

Driscoll, Susan & Diane Gedymin. *Get Published!* New York: iUniverse, Inc. 2006.

Elsom, Jr. Eldridge & Mark Eldridge. *The Obvious Expert*. Heath, MA: MasterMind Publishing, LLC 2004.

Gaughen, Barbara & Ernest Weckbaugh. *Book Blitz*. Burbank, CA: Best-Seller Books 1994.

Holzner, Steven. *Facebook Marketing*. Indianapolis, IN: Que 2009.

Jenkins, Jerrold & Ann Stanton. *Publish to Win*. Traverse, MI: Rhodes & Easton 1997.

Kremer, John. *1001 Ways to Market Your Books*. Fairfield, IA: Open Horizons 1998.

Levinson, Jay, Rick Frishman, & Michael Larsen. *Guerrilla Marketing for Writers*. Cincinnati, OH: Writer's Digest Books 1993.

O'Connor, Richard. *How to Market You & Your Book*. Santa Barbara, CA: Coeur de Lion Books 1996.

Pinskey, Raleigh. *101 Ways to Promote Yourself*. New York: Avon 1997.

Poynter, Dan. *The Self-Publishing Manual*. Santa Barbara, CA: Para Publishing 1996.

Rose, M.J. & Angela Adair-Hoy. *How to Publish and Promote Online*. New York: St. Martin's Griffin 2001.

Ross, Marilyn & Tom Ross. *Jump Start Your Book Sales*. Buena Vista, CA: Communication Creativity 1999.

Smith, Mack & Sara Smith. *How To Self-Publish & Market Your Book*. Houston, TX: U R Gems Group, Inc. 2001.

Yudkin, Marcia. *Freelance Writing for Magazines and Newspapers*. New York: Harper & Row, Publishers 1988.

Glossary

Analysis: Takes research, data, or background information and attempts to evaluate and interpret that information.

Blog: A personal journal written on the Internet with the intention of sharing information or influencing others.

Copyright: The exclusive right of the individual who developed the written content or other intellectual properties.

Creative Non-Fiction: A general term for any non-fiction piece that tells a story, offers insight, or provides entertainment. Many blogs fall into this category based on an author's everyday "ramblings" or "musings."

Feature: Takes a single topic and expands on it through research, analysis, and opinion. Its primary function is to provide information and insight.

How-To: Demonstrates the process required to complete a task or accomplish a goal. Many articles written by ghostwriters are "how-to" in nature.

Inspirational: This is where all the self-help gurus come in. It is a motivational style more than a how-to style, because it gives the reader an uplifting experience.

Interview: A written conversation between two people, usually directed by the interviewer. Most interview writers will edit the conversation for clarity.

Investigation: More extensive research than a feature or analysis. Generally seeks to draw conclusions based on new evidence, or to bolster existing conclusions.

List: Very popular format for web articles and blogs. Just a simple run-down of information, broken into basic, bite-sized pieces.

Memoir: Usually written in first person or in an "as told to" format. Describes in detail the story or specific incidents of the author's life.

News: Primarily for newspapers, newsletters, and some articles. Reports on events as accurately and impartially as possible.

Value: The net bundle of benefits derived by the customer from the product you are selling.

Recommended Readings

Learn about information designed to enhance your professional writing and influence.

Business Management and Strategic Thinking

Microtrends by Mark Penn & Kinney Zalesne

The Portable MBA in Entrepreneurship by William Bygrave & Andrew Zacharakis

Thriving on Chaos by Tom Peters

Visionary Leadership by Burt Nanus

Global Market

Growing Your Business Globally by Robert Taft

International Business by Charles Thomas Friedman

The World is Flat by Thomas Friedman

Marketing Resources

Guerrilla Marketing by Jay Conrad Levinson

Knock Your Socks Off by Jay Conrad Levinson

The Innovator's Dilemma by Clayton Christensen

Sales and Relationship Selling

10 Steps to Sales Success by Tim Breithaupt

Relationship Selling by Jim Cathcart

Sales Success Made Simple by Brian Tracy

Writing and Publishing

101 Ways to Promote Yourself by Raleigh Pinksey

Dojo Wisdom for Writers by Jennifer Lawler

Entrepreneurship by Robert Hisrich, Michael Peters, & Dean Shepherd

Everything You Need to Know to Write, Publish, & Market Your Book by Patrika Vaughn

Get Published by Susan Driscoll & Diane Gedymin

Jump Start Your Book Sales by Marilyn & Tom Ross

Niche Marketing for Writers, Speakers, and Entrepreneurs by Gordon Burgett

Nonfiction Book Proposals Anybody Can Write by Elizabeth Lyon

On Writing Well by William Zinsser

Publishing to Niche Markets by Gordon Burgett

Rules for Writers by Diana Hacker

Self-Publishing Planning by Dick Lutz

Six-Figure Freelancing by Kelly James-Enger

The African American Writer's Handbook by Robert Fleming

The APA Manual

The Self-Publishing Manual by Dan Poynter

The Writer's Market

Writer's Digest

Writing Nonfiction by Dan Poynter

About this Professional Author

Dr. Daryl D. Green is an international blogger, columnist, independent publisher, and a nationally recognized author. Dr. Green loves developing intellectual properties to assist individuals with making better decisions. He has over 20 years of assisting organizations and individuals.

Currently, Dr. Green is the author of several books and writes a syndicated online column on contemporary issues. Over 3,000 online publishers and content providers around the globe have used his articles. His *FamilyVision* column syndicated through the Newspaper Publishers Association reached over 200 newspapers and more than 15 million readers across the country. Additionally, Dr. Green has been noted and quoted by

USA Today, Ebony Magazine, and the *Associated Press.* He has also been a freelance writer and guest columnist for various publications, including *Knoxville News Sentinel, Knoxville Enlightener, Discovery Magazine,* and the *IEEE Technology and Society Magazine,* in addition to being a special assignment reporter for the *BIG Bulletin/Reporter.*

His professional resume includes management, engineering, research and development, marketing, and personal coaching. He received a B.S. in Mechanical Engineering and an M.A. in Organizational Management. Dr. Green also received a doctoral degree in Strategic Leadership from Regent University. He is a former talk show host, a nationally recognized lecturer, nationally syndicated columnist, and personal advisor. Before his 30th birthday, he had already managed over 400 projects, estimated at $100 million dollars. These experiences place him in a unique position for understanding emerging trends.

If you would like Dr. Green to speak with your organization or would like more information about his company services, please contact:

PMLA

P.O. Box 32733

Knoxville, TN 37930-2733

Phone: (865) 602-7858

Email: **pmla@att.net**

Home page: **www.darylgreen.org**

Readers' Suggestions & Input

We are constantly updating our reports so that they are accurate and relevant. If you find missing information, would like to provide suggestions, or have new information relevant to this discussion, please write, fax, or e-mail us at:

PMLA

P.O. Box 32733

Knoxville, TN 37930-2733

Fax: (865) 602-7858

Email: **advice@darylgreen.org**

Other Books by Dr. Green

Dr. Green continues to research and produce information that aims to improve society. Below is a synopsis of some of his other products:

A Call to Destiny: How to Create Effective Ways to Assist Black Boys in America provides a practical assessment of what happens to young black boys in America. It seeks to provide ways for parents, educators, and supporters to assist these boys in their positive development. Without any intervention, young black boys, regardless of their social class, will not survive in the twenty-first century. In this book, A Call to Destiny, you will (a) examine the severity of the problems facing young black boys, (b) learn new strategies to bring solutions to your child and the community at large, and (c) provide inspiration to continue the fight to save this generation. (Paperback: 50 pages, ISBN: 978-1442181021)

Awakening the Talents Within is a powerful, step-by-step approach that individuals can use to solve problems and enhance their overall success. This book is a wake-up call for the next generation of leaders. Dr. Green uses his charismatic style for today's hip-hop culture, dealing with a wide range of issues from stopping procrastination to creating business ownership. The solutions contained in the book reflect over ten years of managing, consulting, and teaching in government, non-profit, business, private, and academic institutions. (Paperback: 136 pages, ISBN: 978-0595146130, Hardcover: 140 pages, ISBN: 978-0595745722)

Book Publishing for Professionals provides the secrets of gaining this useful power. Packed with proven insights and advice, this book provides simple, logical steps for professionals. It includes effective writing tools, the best publishing options, and marketing strategies to make your book successful in the marketplace. It is geared toward the writer who wants to publish a non-fiction book (biography, cookbook, self-help, Christian book, textbook, etc.). (Paperback: 68 pages, ISBN: 978-1449985561, Kindle: 68 pages ASIN: B0047T7DPA, Hardcover: 108 pages, ISBN: 978-0-557-98346-9, DVD: 26 minutes, ASIN: B001FB4Z3G, CD: 26 minutes, ASIN: B004CYFBBS)

Breaking Organizational Ties provides practical strategies for employees attempting to cope in jobs or environments which they hate. While most managers are only concerned with the bottom-line, they leave their employees vulnerable to the casualties of competitive markets. This book will enable readers to (a) learn how to survive and enjoy their time at work even in a hostile environment, (b) gain greater confidence in their ability to grow while in a downsizing organization, and (c) discover the insight to go beyond their limitations by breaking the barriers of self-doubt. (Paperback: 124 pages, ISBN: 978-1450511315)

Don't be an Old Fool: Common Sense & Gratitude is a collection of Dr. Green's syndicated columns through the years. The book offers practical strategies for individuals who desire to make better decisions in their lives by using sound, common-sense approaches. With renewed purpose and direction, individuals will be able to energize themselves for the future. (Paperback: 134 pages, ISBN: 978- 1466236530)

Impending Danger: The Federal Handbook for Rethinking Leadership in the 21st Century provides critical answers regarding how government leaders can reduce partisan bickering by changing the current leadership paradigm. With 40 years worth of experience in the public sector, Dr. Green and his co-author, Dr. Gary Roberts, know what they're talking about. The book provides revelations and insights regarding political strife and the answers that can solve them. (Hardcover: 146 pages, ISBN: 978-1607971382)

More Than a Conqueror: Achieving Personal Fulfillment in Government Service is a message about how to take positive steps in achieving your goals while in government service, although any civilians will be able to benefit from this book. In More than a Conqueror, you will (a) go beyond your self-imposed limitations by breaking the barrier of your self-doubt and (b) protect and cultivate your life in order to bring forth the best you can in your generation. (Paperback: 76 pages, ISBN: 978-0971400887)

My Cup Runneth Over: Setting Goals for Single Parents and Working Couples guides families in setting goals for themselves. Daryl and his wife have first-hand experience on this subject, both working full-time jobs, and raising three active children. This book uses a new management process called Meshing TM. The book is very different from most family books, by focusing more on practical solutions. Dr. Green has used his and his wife's experiences as managers from government, non-profit, and private business sectors to help families — regain control of their lives. Written in an informal, entertaining style, it provides information to families that gives them HOPE. Creatively illustrated with graphics and charts, the book is also indexed for quick reference. It is essential reading for families in search of purpose.

Special Awards: January Book of the Month, The Larry Young Show 1998, Special Black History Award at Atkins Library, Featured on Heaven 600 (The Top Gospel Radio Station in the Country). (Paperback: 108 pages, ISBN: 978-1889745039, Audiobook: 978- 1889745053, Audio CD: ASIN: B001VH787E)

Second Chance presents non-profit organizations with a way to use operations management tools for more efficiency. Non-profit organizations will become better-equipped to assist clients and constituents in meeting their needs. Dr. Green co-authored this book with one of his students. Through the eyes of student Noriko Chapman, readers will be taken on a magical journey of overcoming a difficult situation in operations management and in life. (Paperback: 130 pages, ISBN: 978-1461146070)

Selling by Objectives provides insight on how to create more sales during an economic crisis, using seven key ingredients. The book provides practical solutions that today's organizations can easily digest and implement even in an unstable economy. This book is important not only for sales people, but also for any professional involved in selling goods and services with a desire to be successful in the marketplace. Non-profit organizations, business owners, college students, professors, entrepreneurs, and other sales organizations can benefit from this book. (Paperback: 138 pages, ISBN: 978-1470054342)

Appendices

Appendix A: Samples of Professional Writings

Appendix B: Creating a Publishing Company

Appendix C: Potential Publishing Portals

Appendix A

Sample of Non-Fiction Writing for Professionals

A variety of writing samples are given as non-fiction writing opportunities for professionals. These examples are actual works submitted by students, peers, and myself. The names have been changed to protect privacy. This list is not exhaustive, but provides a good snapshot of how professionals gain more influence. The following written articles are provided:

Academic Article

Advice Column

Article - APA

Blog Article

Blog Comment (response)

Case Study Analysis

Consultant Report

Editorial/Commentary

Employment Letter (pitch)

Guest-Blogger Article

How-To/Instructional Column

Interview (written by Dr. Daryl Green)

Letter to the Editor

Magazine Article

Media release (written by Dr. Daryl Green)

Query letter

Academic Article – APA Style

Running head:
IMPACT OF POSTMODERNISM
ON PUBLIC SECTOR LEADERSHIP

Impact of Postmodernism on Public Sector Leadership

Daryl D. Green
Regent University

ABSTRACT

Purpose – This paper explores contemporary leadership theory within a postmodernism society in the public sector. The paper investigates leadership theory by comparing and contrasting bureaucratic theory, transactional leadership theory, and transformational leadership theory in the ever-changing workforce of federal employees.

Design/Methodology/Approach – Begins by discussing the current contemporary leadership theories and postmodernism. This investigation then explores these concepts by utilizing an extensive literary review of over 20 documents, including scholarly opinions and practitioner discussions.

Findings – Explains the extent to which the cultural changes in society are impacting the future workforce in the public sector. The paper concludes with a set of five strategic implications for researchers and practitioners. This effort contributes to further exploration into understanding leadership and organizational culture in the public sector.

Originality/Value – This paper is an original study of the postmodern movement as it relates to contemporary leadership theories. It uniquely analyzes postmodernism with leadership theory in the unpredictable environment of federal bureaucracy. The study is significant because there are government-wide human capital problems, and this is highly relevant to anyone who must lead in the public sector. Researchers and practitioners interested in the public workforce as it transitions over the next several years will find the postulated concepts intriguing and beneficial.

Article Type: Concept Paper

INTRODUCTION

With 60 percent of the government's 1.6 million employees eligible for retirement, the federal government finds itself in a hostile environment. The changes in workforce demographics will create leadership challenges in the future as Baby Boomer employees make their massive exodus from the workforce. For complementary leaders, there is a caution sign that reads, "Proceed cautiously, danger ahead." Currently, the government has declared its human capital practices as a "high risk" area of concern (Blunt, 2003). Linda Springer, the Office of Personnel Management (OPM) Director, calls this issue a retirement tsunami and feels managers need to start taking this cultural shift seriously (Ziegler, 2006). In the past, corporate culture has been able to stabilize such influences; corporate culture gives employees a blueprint for understanding organizational values and beliefs. What happens to an organization when the leader's values are no longer aligned to the belief system of the employees? Reacting to changing cultural influences and global threats abroad, the federal government finds itself in a major transformation process (Blunt, 2003). These situations are made more complicated due to the massive exodus of its leaders. The leadership training for senior executives has been sparse and inadequate in relationship to these culture changes.

The purpose of this article is to provide an exploratory insight related to leadership theory and its application in the postmodern era. This paper examines several aspects of leadership theory consisting of bureaucratic theory, transactional leadership theory, and transformational leadership theory in the public sector. The primary objective is to identify the current values attributed to contemporary leadership and compare varying leadership theories in the postmodern period. The following discussion will be investigated: (a) the current organizational changes, (b) the postmodern culture and its impact upon the workforce, and (c) understanding leadership theory in the postmodern period. These issues are significant because of the potential conflicts that can exist between leaders and employees in organizations.

CONTEMPORARY LEADERSHIP THEORY

Leadership Theory provides researchers an opportunity to understand leader-follower relationships in a cultural framework. Prewitt (2004) noted that the current leadership theories are based on modernist assumptions and are out of date with leading postmodern organizations. Schmidt (2006) argued that leadership definitions reflect the viewpoint of an industrial society, and a new era begat a new definition for leadership. Nevertheless, this paper defines leadership as a contextual influence that has an impact on subordinates' attitudes and performance through effects on the subordinates' perceptions of their job characteristics (Northouse, 2004). Therefore, leaders have the capacity to influence the values needed in a changing organizational environment (Ferguson, 2003).

POSTMODERN CULTURE

Postmodernism is a philosophical term with a cultural context. Modernism places man at the center of reality by utilizing science to explain the meaning of life. In contrast, postmodernism places no one at the center of reality and has no core explanation of life (Kelm, 1999). Ingraffia (1995) figuratively described modernism as an attempt to elevate man into God's place while postmodernism seeks to destroy the very place and attributes of God. Some of the key themes of postmodernism include (a) Pluralism, which means the denial of any one universal truth; (b) Non-objectivism, which conveys that all facts are not hard facts and science has limited application; (c) Deconstruction, which teaches that meaning is through the interpreter rather than the text or object interpreted; (d) Cynicism/pessimism, which promotes the absence of absolute truth, no universal purpose in life, and no possibility of arriving at certain knowledge of anything; and (e) Community, which advocates meaning and understanding determined through a tribal or community setting (Kelm, 1999). Therefore, postmodernism provides a conceptual threat to traditional organizations.

METHODOLOGY

This investigation provides exploratory data by utilizing an extensive literary review of over 20 documents including scholarly opinions and practitioner discussions. The contributions made by well-known researchers in the fields of postmodernism and leadership theory, such as Bass and Yukl, were investigated. The primary objective of this review of literature is to increase depth of knowledge in this field in order to make a relevant analysis of each theory. This is surprisely very little research related to the most effective leadership style needed to deal with the postmodern generation.

Electronic databases such as EBSCO Host and the Internet were searched using key words 'leadership theories,' bureaucracy,' 'transactional leadership,' 'transformational leadership,' 'organizational values,' 'corporate culture,' and 'postmodernism.' There was a significant absence of literature related to leadership theories as it relates to postmodernism. Through this process, there is an opportunity to discover the gaps in research.

DISCUSSION AND ANALYSIS

Amoeba-like Organizational Change

The enormous demographic changes within the 21st century American workforce are creating organizational growth pains. For the first time in American history, there will be four generations co-existing in the workplace (Hankin, 2005). With global competition, a tightening of corporate budget, and threats of outsourcing core organizational functions, leaders cannot afford to manage in the traditional fashion. Currently, there is considerable buzz among practitioners and academics on the role of leadership theory and organizational culture in organizational performance. Harding (2000) explained that a new generation of workers will produce significant human resource problems for traditional organizations. He described this new generation as the *Emergent Workforce*, which crosses age groups, gender, race, and geography (Harding, 2000). This new set of workers is driven by a new set of values and job expectations. For example, Emergent employees are viewed as job hoppers. In one study, Emergent employees (88%) believed that loyalty was not related to employment length while Traditional employees (94%) viewed loyalty as the willingness to stay with an employer for the long term (Harding, 2000).

Another key value shift among generations is their priorities. While Baby Boomer males and previous generations were more work-focused, Generation X and Y employees are more family-focused.

Younger generations are also less accepting of traditional gender roles than previous generations (Harding, 2000). This Emergent Workforce also seeks a more spiritual workplace that emphasizes personal integrity and accountability (Hankin, 2005). Clearly, these differences in value systems create communication barriers and can result in an unproductive organization (Washington, 2002). Thus, the Emergent Workforce becomes more complicated to manage because its members are often motivated by different leadership styles as shown in Table 1 (Hackman & Johnson, 2004).

Table 1. Characteristics of the Emergent Workforce

Generation	Leadership Preference
The Matures (1927- 1945)	As a follower -Thrive under a directive leadership style As a leader -Lead others by taking charge and making decisions alone
Baby Boomers (1946-1964)	As a follower -Thrive under a participatory leadership style As a leader -Lead in a collegial and consensual fashion with a general concern of others Source: *Leadership: A Communication Perspective* by Hackman & Johnson
Generation X (1965 -1976)	As a follower –Does not thrive under authority leadership style As a leader -Lead others by being adaptable to change, fair, competent, participatory, and diversity-sensitive
Generation Y (1977 – present)	As a follower - Does not thrive under authority leadership style As a leader -Lead with a tolerance of others, value-centered, rule-oriented, and culturally sensitive Source: *Leadership: A Communication Perspective* by Hackman & Johnson

A Clash of Cultural Values

As organizations continue to replace employees under this changing environment, traditional organizational values will be challenged by postmodern values. Economic, social, and political influences have impacted the value system of today's workforce (Wren, 1994). Organizations communicate their expectations both formally and informally through their corporate culture. Scholars call this environment organizational culture. In most businesses, organizational culture has been a domain where institutions try to promote the values of a more efficient and effective organization. Schultz (1992) argued, however, that postmodernism challenges the very assumptions of the merits of corporate culture. First, postmodernism questions the assumption of the goodness of such corporate values. It transforms these corporate icons into hollow rituals (Schultz, 1992). Second, postmodernism questions corporate culture as an effective tool for organizational identity. Postmodern advocates view corporate culture as producing carbon copies of the same culture in different organizations; this situation effaces the last remains of the organizational originality (Schultz,

1992). Lastly, postmodernism rejects the premise that corporate values can regulate employee behaviors through meaningful events and internalized knowledge. It replaces this organization assumption with the seductiveness of corporate culture to act through aesthetics, renewal, and modern illusions (Schultz, 1992). These postmodernism premises attack the heart of traditional organizations and thus, provide an avenue for organizational conflict between leaders and followers. Malphurs (2004) explained that organizational values co-exist on two levels, personal and corporate. On a personal level, individuals in general have a set of core values that dictate how they respond to a situation. At the corporate level, every organization has a set of core values that guides the organization while it does business. Organizational values are a key component of its character and signal to followers the organization's bottom-line (Malphurs, 2004). Conversely, an individual's value system will help determine a person's involvement in an organization or a cause. A well-informed employee who understands his own value should align himself with a similar minded organization (Malphurs, 2004). However, the problem arises when the employee's values do not align with the organization. Hackman and Johnson (2004) explained that leaders and followers are also interrelated. For example, Admiral Gunn has very liberal opinions on social issues more than his fellow officers. However, Admiral Gunn must promote the organizational values of the Navy with which he may personally disagree. How does Admiral Gunn promote corporate values to his followers in which he does not believe?

At this moment in time, an organizational conflict is brewing. Today, many organizations operate under a modern cultural cloud while the vast majority of new employees operate in a postmodern culture. Leaders exert a great amount of influence in guiding their followers although followers are more involved in implementing the organizational objectives. A leader's behavior is also influenced by cultural values and tradition (Yukl, 2002). Organ and Bateman (1991) suggested that the existence of a hierarchy, competition, and constraints on behavior guarantee that frustration will be frequent in an organization. Malphurs (2004) maintained that congruent values are the answer to these value conflicts. In mixing modern and postmodern values in organizations, incongruent values are generated (Malphurs, 2004). Therefore, there will be conflicting values held by the modern organization and the competing values espoused by the Emergent Workforce in the postmodern period. This creates chaos (Malphurs, 2004). For example, postmodernism is multi-cultural and promotes social tolerance. The media heavily bombards today's workforce with these impressions. The casual observer may not observe anything from these media influences; however, organizational leaders can not afford to underestimate these culture changes. Postmodern influences are clearly seen in urban subculture where its followers are characterized by (a) questioning everything, (b) viewing truth as relative, (c)valuing relationships over institutions, (d) valuing the ability of storytelling, and (e) demonstrating of emotion and experience (Smith & Jackson, 2005). Therefore, organizational leaders will need to be real, relevant, and respectful to gain credibility with this subculture (Smith & Jackson, 2005).

Analyzing Leadership Theory in a Culture Quagmire

Applying varying leadership theories in a postmodern workplace could produce a cultural quagmire for organizations. Malphurs (2004) argued that a leader's values influence his followers greatly even though leadership is an amoral process. He further noted that leaders often mirror the organizational values and shape employee values by modeling the way (Malphurs, 2004). Kouzes and Posner (1995) argued that leaders make visions and values meaningful to followers by modeling the way. Much of the assumption about the leader's values is that it is a constant; however, leaders as well as organizations go through a process of value formulation, which may cause a state of flux (Malphurs, 2004). Postmodernism also influences leaders as well as employees, organizations and leaders take longer for these changes to take place; therefore, leaders and organizations are relatively fixed (Malphurs, 2004). Hackman and Johnson (2004) argued that leaders find themselves as negotiators when incompatible interest comes into play and forces leaders to seek a cooperative climate where both parties can agree. However, the competing interest of a modern organization and a postmodern workplace makes this difficult for leaders. Therefore, a new leadership paradigm in organizations needs to be analyzed under continual postmodern influences. Schmidt (2006) advocated a new type of leader in the postmodern age. He describes a leader who understands that many things can not be analyzed away by science. Schmidt also insisted that this leader needs principles based on character and integrity where postmodernism creates a world without rules (Schmidt, 2006, pg.2). According to Prewitt (2004), current leadership in large bureaucratic organizations is invalid for a postindustrial society. It is invalid because it assumes a rational workplace where a bureaucratic structure is sustainable (Prewitt, 2004). However, in the postmodern age, organizations are often complex, networked, emotional, and chaotic.

Understanding leadership theory in postmodernism is vital because leaders are responsible for discovering and articulating the organization's primary values (Malphurs, 2004). Yukl (2002) explained that most leadership theories are focused on processes at only one level because it is difficult to develop a multilevel theory for all situations. Vickrey (n.d.) argued that communications is critical for effective leaders and can explain why some leaders are better than their peers with similar followers. There are concerns, however, about the power of leaders in organizations to influence the values of followers. Yukl (2002) explained that scholars worry about the misuse of power and control over information to bias follower perceptions which could be perceived as attempting to change the underlying values and beliefs of followers. Likewise, the Emergent Workforce requires more collaboration, social intelligence, and worker participation in order to maintain sustainability. Thus, this investigation analyzes three current leadership theories that may be found in public organizations and forecast the impacts of postmodernism influences.

Each theory has it own unique characteristics. First, the leadership theories are Bureaucratic Theory, Transactional Leadership Theory, and Transformational Leadership Theory. In the 1900s, Max Weber postulated that a manager's authority in an organization should be based not on tradition or charisma but on the position held by managers in the organization hierarchy (Wren, 1994). Weber's ideas formed the basis of what is known today as Bureaucracy Theory. In a bureaucratic structure, large organizations such as governments and religious institutions can control employees by giving leader legitimate power and standardizing work processes. The federal government is a form of bureaucracy.

Therefore, many outsiders view organizational leaders as bureaucrats. This title is not viewed as a positive attribute in society. The elements of a bureaucracy include: (a) authority and responsibility clearly identified and

135

legitimatized, (b) hierarchy of authority producing a chain of command, (c) leaders selected by technical competency, training, or education, (d) leaders appointed, not elected, (e) administrative officials work for fixed salaries and have no ownership of process or organization, (f) Administrators subject to strict rules for control (Wren, 1994). Although Weber viewed these attributes as positives during his time, societal changes and economic pressures have shifted public opinion on the merits of bureaucratic theory in a postmodern culture. Bureaucratic leaders influence employees primarily on their legality of authority and the right to issue commands (Bass, 1990). Clearly, these assumptions maintained by bureaucratic leaders will create a value crisis for members in a postmodern workforce.

The process of bureaucracy is often viewed as a cold and heartless process to postmodern employees. For example, a government office manager may work in an environment where she is not respected or valued because of her pay grade. She is never given special assignments or career development activities. She soon grows tired of asking to be treated fairly and becomes a robot in her job. This is a tragic situation because this office manager is special. In her private life, she serves as the chairperson for her local nonprofit organization and is highly respected in her community because of her leadership abilities. Unfortunately, the employee's worth is seen through the len of an impersonal process. Some of the problems with a bureaucracy include the impersonal rules, absoluteness of leadership in authority, and the enforcement of standardization and conformity on individualism (RevisionNotes.Co.Uk, 2001). Organizational leaders need to analyze the ramification of bringing these postmodern employees into a non-flexible bureaucracy.

Second, many effective managers still utilize Transactional Leadership Theory in order to obtain organizational objectives. Transactional leadership along with transformational leadership was advocated by Burns, a political sociologist, in order to link the relationship between leader and follower (Northouse, 2004). In the Transactional Leadership Theory, leadership involves the exchange of benefits. While the leader provides a benefit to followers, in exchange followers comply by achieving the leader's desired outcomes (Jin, n.d.). The leader-follower relationship is submerged in self-interest. The followers enjoy the benefit of extrinsic and intrinsic rewards while the leader obtains status, the privileges of authority, influence, prestige, or other management benefits (Bass, 1990). Critics argue that transactional leaders are most concerned with satisfying the physical needs of the employees and do not want to disrupt the status quo (Hackman & Johnson, 2004). For example, Bill is a survivor of massive downsizing in his company. Because of this fact, his managers give Bill plenty of overtime to get the job down. However, Bill is unhappy because he is doing the work of several people. Bill never does anything extra from the organization because he feels the company does not care.

Transactional leadership also depends upon management by exception and negative feedback; it is an advantage as long as the employee is a rational and economic being (McAulay, 2003). Therefore, these values do not align themselves well to the needs of postmodern employees who are searching for a meaningful existence. Finally, the Transformational Theory also provides an effective method of exchange between leader and followers. In contrast to Transactional Leadership Theory, Transformational Leadership Theory speaks to the higher needs of employees. Whereas transactional leaders work within the framework of the self interest of his or her employees, transformational leaders seek to change the framework

(Bass, 1990). A transformational leader will request employees to transcend their own self interests for the good of organization and focus on long-term benefits rather than short-term gain (Bass, 1990). Unlike transactional leadership, transformational leadership attempts to develop employees in such a manner to reach for high performance without the carrot of reward or reprimand. Bass argues that transformational leaders, however, augment some of the attributes of transactional leaders on the efforts, satisfaction, and effectiveness of employees (Bass, 1990). Transformational leaders attempt to raise the consciousness of his followers (Bass, 1990). These attributes work well with postmodern employees. In spite of this positive outlook, transformational leadership has its problem with postmodernism. First, transformational leaders in the federal government still operate in a bureaucratic system that is highly inflexible. Second, transformational leaders are social architects of their organizations so that they promote organizational values and norms to employees (Northouse, 2004). Some postmodernists would consider this negative since these leaders often influence and shape employee attitudes for the organization's benefit. Other scholars argue that transformational leadership is elitist and antidemocratic

139

(Northouse, 2004). Similar to other theories, Transformational Leadership Theory has its drawback when applying postmodern concept. For example, Kelly, a federal executive, created a charged workplace environment for his employees. The workforce loved his charismatic ways. However, his fellow managers demonstrate unethical conduct. While Kelly encourages his employees to have high ethical behavior, he is silent on his peers. By supporting this corporate culture, Kelly loses the trust of his postmodern workforce.

Finally, Schmidt (2006) explained that the postmodern leader should have the following characteristics: (a) adaptable, (b) spiritual-focus, (c) tolerance for ambiguity in life, (d) entrepreneurial in his approach, (e) service-oriented, (f) accountable for action, (g) life-long learners, (h) upgrading performance, and (i) participatory. Although there are many positive attributes of contemporary leadership theories, organizational leaders should be cautious with implementing them in a postmodern framework.

CONCLUSION

Organizational leaders in the public sector will find new challenges as they begin to replace their present workforce in this Postmodern Era. The paper demonstrated that there is an impending public crisis as postmodernism makes its impacts on this traditional framework. Influences of postmodernism make the Emergent Workforce more cynical and pessimistic about life. Postmodernism has employees debating on what is morally right. Therefore, organizational leaders must operate against a backdrop of postmodernism where followers are untrusting of corporate culture. Organizational leaders, who ignore or dismiss the impact of these cultural changes, may find themselves managing a chaotic situation.

Through this investigation, an analysis was conducted comparing aspects of leadership theories to postmodernism. The paper argues that each of the leadership theories have some flaws when applied to postmodernism. Further empirical research needs to be conducted on the influence of postmodernism on leaders, the workforce, and organizational performance. The insight gained through this research may lead to better management strategies for handling a transitional workforce in the public sector. This effort contributes to further exploration into understanding leadership and organizational culture in the public sector.

STRATEGIC IMPLICATIONS

The following strategic implications emerged as a resulted of this investigation and are offered to assist organizations with transitioning an Emergent Workforce into their organizations:

1. Communicate formally and informally the organizational values to employees on a routine basis. Hackman and Johnson (2004) explained that leaders exert a great degree of influence in an organization; therefore, leaders must have more responsibility for the overall direction of the organization.

2. Demand that managers model those corporate values to followers in the organization. Kouzes and Posner (1995) explained that leaders must lead by example so that employees can see they are committed.

3. Discuss organizational values with recruits in the early stage of interviewing to determine if their values align themselves with organizational values.

4. Train current managers so that they understand the needs of this Emergent Workforce. Linda Springer, the OPM Director, feels that managers need to be aware of generational traits because differences in work attitude and style can pose challenges (Ziegler, 2006).

5. Establish an intern program at your workplace where new employees can connect to the organization. Encourage interns to seek out mentors. Discuss the various leadership styles and allow workers to get a sample of each from current leadership.

REFERENCES

Bass, B., 1999, *Bass & Stogdill's handbook of leadership*, The Free Press, New York.

Blunt, R., 2003, "*Leaders growing leaders: preparing the next generation of public service executives,*" Human Capital Management Series.

Ferguson, C., 2003, "*Whose vision? whose values? on leading information services in an era of persistent change,*" [Online], Retrieved on March 7, 2006, Available at **http://www.clir.org/pubs/reports/pub123/ferguson.html**.

Hackman, M. & Johnson, C., 2000. *Leadership: A communication perspective*, Waveland Press, Long Grove, IL.

Hankin, H., 2005, "*Can we recognize our future employees,*" Workspan, vol. 48, no. 9, pp.12-13.

Harding, K., 2000, "*Understanding emerging workforce trends,*" [Online], Retrieved on January 6, 2006, Available at **http://www.dinet/article.php?article_id=129**.

Ingraffia, B., 1995, "*Postmodern theory and biblical theology,*" About Postmodernism. [Online], Retrieved on March 7, 2006, Available at **http://www.freewaybr.com/pomoessay.htm**.

Jin, D. (n.d.), "*Leadership and followership,*" [Online], Retrieved on March 8, 2006, Available at **http://www.dickinson.edu/~jin/Leadership.html**.

Kelm, P., 1999, "*Understanding and addressing a postmodern culture,*" Presented to the Board for Parish Services.

Kouzes, J. & Posner, B., 1995, *The leadership challenge*, Jossey-Bass Publishers, San Francisco.
Malphurs, A., 2004. *Values-driven leadership*, Bakerbooks, Grand Rapids, MI.

McAulay, L., 2003, "Transformational leadership: a response to limitations in conventional information systems evaluation," Electronic Journal of Information Systems Evaluation.

Northouse, P., 2004, *Leadership theory and practice*, Sage Publications, Thousand Oaks, CA.

Organ, D. & Bateman, T., 1991, *Organizational behavior*, Irwin, Homewood, IL.

Prewitt, V., 2004, *"Integral leadership for the 21st century,"* World Futures, vol. 60, 327-333.

Revision-notes.co.uk., 2001, *"Characteristics of bureaucracy,"* [Online], Received on March 8, 2006, Available at **http://www.revision-notes.co.uk/revision/1019.html**.

Schmidt, H., 2006, *"Leadership in a postmodern world,"* [Online], Retrieved on March 7, 2006, Available at **http://www.mbseminary.edu/current/images/article/schmidt1.htm**.

Schultz, M., 1992, *"Postmodern picture of culture,"* Int. Studies of Mgt. & Org., vol. 22, no. 2, pp. 15-35.

Smith, E. & Jackson, P., 2005, *The hip hop church*, IVP Press, Downers Grove, IL.

Vickrey, J. (n.d.), *"Symbolic leadership: The symbolic nature of leadership,"* [Online], Received on March 7, 2006, Available at **http://www.au.af.mil/au/awc/awcgate/au-24/vickrey.pdf#search='article%2C%20symbolic%20leadership%2C%20jim%20vickrey**.

Washington, G., 2002, *"Staffing the postmodern army,"* Combined Arms Center Military Review, pp. 1-7.

Yukl, G., 2002. *Leadership in organizations*, Pearson Education, Inc., Delhi, India.

Ziegler, M., March, 6, 2006, *"OPM chief urges new vision to recruit younger feds,"* Federal Times, 6.

Advice Column

Marriage is a Crazy Love

Summary: Examine genuine love in marriage that is different than popular culture.

Introduction

The buzz rang across the world. The word was finally out, "Whitney Houston was dead." The idea that a woman so talented would be forever lost to the world was unthinkable. On February 12, 2012, Whitney Houston had died at the age of 48 years old. Through the public eyes, the six-time Grammy winner was on a sobriety roller-coaster. In her awarding song, Whitney sings, "If I should stay I would only be in your way, so I'll go. But I know I'll think of you every step of the way. And I...will always love you." Yet, this kind of love is mysterious. In a world looking for comfort from Whitney's death, there are some lessons to learn for everyone. The article examines today's marriages and how to assess true love.

Marriage Drama

Many people blame Whitney's eventual downfall of her stormy marriage. She married Bobby Brown in 1992. With her concert cancellations and erratic behavior, rumors circulated about her drug abuse with husband Bobby Brown. On one occasion, police responded to a domestic violence call from Whitney about her husband. Bobby was eventually charged with misdemeanor battery in 2003 for he allegedly striking his wife in a heated domestic altercation.

In 2005, the couple allowed the world to take an inside peek into their rocky relationship with a reality TV show Being Bobby Brown. Whitney later admitted to Oprah Winfrey in an interview that doing the show was a mistake. She did the show to support her husband Bobby. In an interview, Whitney explained, "Nobody makes me do anything I don't wanna do, it's my decision. So the biggest devil is me. I'm either my best friend or my worst enemy."

After 14 years of marriage, Whitney and Bobby ended their marriage in 2007, but not all the drama associated with being famous. In fact, drug addiction continued to haunt Whitney's life. Her daughter Bobbi Kristina, who was informally Whitney's primary caretaker, was very close to her mother. Sadly, Whitney and Bobby's marriage will not be remembered for its intense passion, but for its drama and crazy love.

Marriage Problems

The state of marriage should be troubling to many. According to estimates, 46% of women aged 15-44 years were married or 9% were co-habiting which refers to a man and woman living together in a sexual relationship without being married. For men, 42% were married and 9% co-habited. Although many discuss the plight of marriage with about half ending in divorce, marriage continues to provide some stability for families in society. According to a 2002 National Survey of Family Growth by Paula Goodwin, William Mosher, and Anjani Chandra, marriages last longer than co-habiting unions (78% of marriage lasted 1 year or more, compared with less than 30% of co-habitations).

Crazy Love

On a steady pace, popular legends and media experts seek to bombard negativism about traditional marriage as a failing institution. Genuine love in marriage could be a crazy love to individuals caught up in fake love. This unconditional love is best outlined biblically: "Love is patient, love is kind. It does not envy, it does not boast, it is not proud. It is not rude, it is not self-seeking, it is not easily angered, it keeps no record of wrongs." This love is considered a crazy love because it is unconditional. In most marriages, the relationship is transactional. If one person does something, there is a reciprocal action.

Pastor Richard Brown, who routinely offers advice to married and engaged couples, understands the misconceptions that many people have when they enter into marriage. Many expectations are unrealistic. Pastor Brown explains, "Most times our love is conditional. It is about how we act...Saying

'I do' is the easy part. Making a marriage work is the difficult part."

Yet, some of the longest marriages involve more. With people married for over 40 and 50 years, there is more of an effort to accept each other faults and attempt to make the marriage work in spite of the problems. This unselfish marriage strategy is often short-changed with a mindset that marriage is about "Me": my needs must be met.

Conclusion

Whitney Houston will forever be remembered for her powerful voice and lasting memories of unforgettable ballads such as I Will Always Love You. Like Whitney, many people are caught of a marriage roller coaster that ends in their peril. As popular culture replaces the tenets of marriage, lasting marriages are based on genuine love.

Many marriages are filled with drama and unrealistic expectations; some would declare it is a crazy love. However, this is not the same kind of unconditional love that the world argues is a crazy love because it is unconditional. In order to endure the cultural wars, there needs to be the right kind of love that is not transactional or shallow. Let us hope that it is not too late.

© 2012 by Daryl D. Green

About the Expert:

Dr. Daryl Green provides motivation, guidance, and training for leaders at critical ages and stages of their development. He has over 20 years of management experience and has been noted and quoted by USA Today, Ebony Magazine, and Associated Press. For more information, you can go to nuleadership.wordpress.com or **www.darylgreen.org** .

(Available on monthly on NMP Information Services Website as Expert)

Article (Popular Press) – APA Style

Your Child Is A Gymnast & A Manager by **KEISHA BENTLEY**

Performing a double-full-twist is an example of innovation, procedure, and efficiency. I bet you never knew gymnastics could relate to Operations Management. For several years I have taught gymnastics to boys and girls ranging from 2 to 18 years old. Watching a child become proficient in gymnastics is an example of a transformational process. "Transformational learning is defined as learning that induces more far-reaching change in the learner than other kinds of learning, especially learning experiences which shape the learner and produce a significant impact, or paradigm shift, which affects the learner's subsequent experiences (Cooper, 2001)." A transformational process is defined as a user of resources to transform inputs into some desired outputs. An input is everything you need to make a product or service. The output is the result (Jacobs, Chase, & Aquilano, 2009). The inputs in this situation would be the practice, time, effort, money spent for lessons, and dedication to the sport. The outputs are anything from a forward roll to a "series", which consists of a combination of complicated gymnastics stunts performed sequentially.

A "series" is a good example of a process on its own. A series begins with a short run, followed by a round-off, which is followed by a choice of back-handsprings, tucks, twists, or layouts. It is ended with a gymnastics stance, by which the gymnast lands on both feet and then steps back with one foot while raising both hands in the air. Start to finish, the process lasts anywhere from 5 seconds to a minute. The gymnast has to be efficient during the play. If she does not get a powerful run in the beginning, the entire routine will suffer. She has to ensure that she is squatting low enough in each preparation to get a sizeable jump to ensure enough time to flip in the air before reaching the floor. Much time is spent on perfecting these processes. Gymnasts earn scholarships and even Olympic medals for their precise execution of processes. The next time you look at a gymnast, you can think of him or her as a Process Manager.

Companies compete on competitive dimensions. Selling gymnastics lessons is no different. We compete on quality. Our students learn technical skills in a sequential order, without being progressed until the current level of skill is satisfied. The cycle time for each student to progress to the next level is typically one school year. Most of our students perform for competitive cheerleading squads and/or cheer for high school squads. Productivity is a common measure on how well resources are being used. In the broadest sense, it can be defined as outputs divided by inputs (Jacobs, Chase, & Aquilano, 2009). To be useful, there needs to be a baseline. The best indicator of success is benchmarking previous results of our own school. By having a long history in the business, as far as gymnastics is concerned, we are able to judge exactly how many students we should have (capacity), how many should be performing at each level (productivity), and what we need to be doing to improve each area (measures of efficiency). Any indicator of slack is dealt with quickly because it only takes one child lagging in a class to pull the rest down. This child may be referred to as a bottleneck. The only bottleneck allowed in our gym is a cold Root Beer after practice.

References:

Jacobs, F, Chase, R, & Aquilano, N. (2009). Operations and supply management. New York, NY: McGraw-Hill/Irwin.

Cooper, Sunny. "Transformational Learning", November, 2001. No longer available online.

Published at Amazines.com

http://www.amazines.com/article_detail.cfm/3135062?articleid=3135062&title=Operations%2CManagement%2CTransformational%2CProcess%2CInput%2COutput%2CProcess%2CCycle%2CTime%2CProductivity%2CBenchmarking%2CEfficiency

Article Posted: 07/27/2011

Article Views: 76

Articles Written: 2 - MORE ARTICLES FROM THIS AUTHOR

Word Count: 597

Article Votes: 1

Blog Article

In the 1957 classic movie *Desk Set*, the technology revolution begins. The movie takes place at the "Federal Broadcasting Network." Bunny Watson (**Katharine Hepburn**), is responsible for researching and answering questions at the organization's library. With a merger pending, the company looks to automation. In fact, organization ordered two **computers** called "Electronic Brains." Richard Sumner (**Spencer Tracy**), the computer inventor, is brought into the network in order to phase out the library functions in lieu of the human staff. Bunny Watson fights to demonstrate the value of her human existence.

In a hypercompetitive environment, many businesses are outsourcing major functions rather than perform them in-house. Today's businesses have built elaborate systems for better efficiency and effectiveness. Of course, they are driven by the quest for increasing profitability. Robert Jacobs, Richard Chase, and Nicholas Aquilano, authors of *Operations & Supply Management*, suggest that operations management has been a key element in the improvement in productivity in businesses across the world. Many times executive focus on the major expense to operate – labor.

It's a simple equation: productivity equals outputs divided by inputs. If organizations can reduce their inputs for their operations, they can increase output (more profit). Therefore, companies seek to reduce their inputs to generate greater profit. Two of the chief strategies are to outsource non-core functions abroad and to add new technologies for efficiency. These strategies are aimed at reducing labor costs, primarily people. Since 2000, over 3 million U.S. jobs in the manufacturing sector have been moved abroad to countries like China, India, and Korea. Yet, few executives worry about the aftermath of outsourcing initiatives. The remaining workforce is shell-shocked and stressed since they are required to do the work of the laid off workforce. Sadly, many supervisors feel that these workers should be happy to have a job.

Gareth Jones and Jennifer George, authors of *Contemporary Management*, maintain that one of the most important resources in all organizations is the human capital component. Many people wonder if American's businesses cannot compete in manufacturing and other high tech industries, will they forever forgo the Great American Dream for next generation of workers.

How do organizations stimulate their workers while outsourcing key components of their organizations abroad for greater efficiencies?

Published on Nuleadership Revolution Blog

Blog Comment

(from Dean McCann on Blog Topic)

Dr. Green and I have researched the topic of leadership and the green economy. We discovered that little research exists in how the green economy will impact contemporary organizations' strategy, structure, and culture; new theories may need to be developed to assist organizations in developing the right kind of leadership for the green economy; the creation of green jobs may infuse organizations with more emphasis on values and leadership competency; the over dependence on technology to create jobs and sustain society's quality of life carries unintended consequences; and agrarian leadership may offer organizations a better ability to lead workers in the green economy (Green and McCann, 2011).

Green energy is just one of many tools for helping our globe solve its sustainability challenges. However, leaders must first adopt a new leadership model for today's green economy. They need a model that considers sustainability as a cornerstone requirement and helps organizations answer the following questions:

What is sustainable leadership? How can you become a sustainable leader? Will being a sustainable leader bring more profits to your organization? These questions and more should be asked of our top leaders in non-profit organizations to top public companies. They could share their wisdom in forums, such as this blog, and share life lessons that help their business, career, and lives.

Sustainable leadership is concerned with creating current and future profits for an organization while improving the lives of all concerned (McCann and Holt, 2010). Today's organizational leaders must successfully guide their organizations through today's volatile economic times and do so in a sustainable manner

McAslan and Ruberstein (2010) offer recommendations to promote sustainability. These principles of sustainability promote the kind of change that manufacturers should adopt. They will help current manufacturing concerns survive and new manufacturing organizations grow and develop new products required by the global economy. These ten recommendations are presented in the following paraphrased version:

1. Make optimal use of human and material resources in the production process.
2. Provide rewards and incentives to all employees to be more efficient in the use of materials, and human talent in a gain sharing manner.
3. Create disincentives for employees and managers who do not effectively promote sustainability and reach targets.
4. Create and support a culture that promotes sustainability in everything that manufacturing does.
5. Reengineer the business plan that involve adopting new technologies,

human resource systems, and financial reporting that ensure sustainability efforts are cost effective and promote profitability.

6. Incorporate externalities in business decisions. Consider things that the company may not be charged for, such as pollution, but should consider as part of the sustainability plan.

7. Demand real progress immediately and increase it in a cumulative manner as the manufacturing organization learns to be sustainable.

8. Develop plans in three phases for the sustainability effort: 1-3 years, 4-10, and ten to twenty years for achieving optimal use of material and human resources.

9. Demand and expect that the supply chain used by the manufacturing organization adopt and implement sustainability planning and implementation.

10. Integrate sustainability into the marketing, public relations, reputation, product development, and transportation processes of the company. (pp. 3-4)

Regards,

Jack McCann, Dean of the Lincoln Memorial University School of Business at Harrogate, TN

References

Green, D. D. & McCann, J. (2011). Benchmarking a leadership model for the green economy. Benchmarking: An International Journal, Vol. 18 Iss: 3, pp.445 – 465.

Published on Nuleadership Revolution Blog

Case Study Analysis

Global or National: Health or Medical Company

PHILIPS

(Notable Brand Portfolio)

MBA 511

K2-groupB-Global Healthcare case -9-2010

Group Name: LMU-2010FA-MBA-511-K Group B

Date: 9/9/2010

Group B Members: M. F., S. H., L. H., D. P.

Executive Summary

Philips Electronics is a large company that employs over 36,000 people worldwide. The Philips portfolio holds 3 major divisions of Consumer Electronics, Lighting, and Healthcare products with recognizable brands such as Norelco and Magnavox. Philips strategically entered the Healthcare industry in 1994 by focusing on high magnet technologies, and has since seen excellent returns and tremendous growth. Healthcare quickly became the #1 priority in the portfolio, while using the Philips name in electronics and lighting as its publicity and advertising tool.

Philips Healthcare supplies large products such as MRI units, CV systems, and X-ray machines from their European manufacturing facilities. Because of their size, coordination among several groups has to be accurate. A member of Philips US Supply Chain Project Management team, Joe Pajcic, was interviewed to provide insight on the inputs involved for a successful delivery of these units and the need for continuous improvements.

Analysis

This analysis looked at the strategic planning for Philips Logistic Supply Chain in the movement of the Healthcare products. Several of these products are very large and take a high level of coordination to complete a successful delivery. MRI units weigh as much as 25,000lbs (15,000lbs magnets and 10,000lbs support systems). CV systems are between 10-15,000lbs, and X-rays being around 6,000lbs. While the magnets are the primary technology focus behind most units, they are also the largest and most sensitive. Once the units are manufactured, the magnets are "charged" and stored with a low degree helium mix. If there are any delays during delivery and installation, the team could lose the "charge." If this occurs the magnets must be shipped back to the manufacturing plant for recharging, and could potentially become worthless. Each magnet ranges between $1-2.5 million in value.

The inputs start with setting guidelines for Healthcare deliveries, and mapping out the supply chain path from factory to hospital. Their outputs consist of a complete delivery and installation, reviewing delivery issues with the carriers, doing root cause analysis, and corrective action for problem deliveries. Several calls are established to make sure all groups are aligned for delivery. Initial moving crews, forwarders, engineers, the customer, and secondary moving crews all have to be in place at the right time to ensure a complete and perfect delivery. Also, specialized tools have to arrive with the moving crews to ensure the large units can be moved.

Healthcare systems are general within hospital standards with many available options. The units become a "build to suit" type of factory operation with a basic platform. Once the factory ship date is determined, the project management team takes over and decides on the mode of transport (expedited or not). The next significant date is the receipt at the dock or airport, customs clearance, and FDA clearance. The system is then ready to ship to the moving crew and engineers for delivery. Any issues along the supply chain (i.e., labor shortage, force majeure) can lead to expedite charges that can escalate very quickly. The project management team keeps constant dialogue with the customer to make sure the delivery date is intact. If for any reason the hospital cannot take the unit, Philips is forced to put the unit on life support as to not lose the "charge".

The team measures (at time of site delivery) what Philips calls the "Perfect Delivery." They need the CV, MRI, CT, Nuc Med, or X-ray system to deliver as scheduled, on time, with the proper moving crew and tools. These tools include items such as forklifts, pallet jacks, cordless screwdrivers, floor protectant, among others. Philips is responsible for any damage that occurs at the customer's site for not using the proper tools. This team also measures the effectiveness of the factory, the ocean/air forwarder, the ocean/air carrier, as well as the "last mile" moving crew. Their goal for perfect deliveries is 95-98% "on-time." Damage measurements are taken for each, as well as more subjective surveys, particularly with the customers involved. For some jobs, the units are too big to move down hallways, and therefore have to be inserted through holes cut from the engineers.

The issues and concerns that Philips has are that hospital deliveries must be precise. They must be on time with the right people, and with the right tools. Obviously, R&D must keep up with innovations throughout the market to keep Philips competitive. Some recent issues have arisen with customs and FDA as they have input stricter regulations and employed more people to oversee their implementation. Also, ocean and air carriers have made changes to their services due to the poor economy, which effectively lengthened Philips shipping lead-times.

Conclusion/Recommendation

In looking at the analysis, the feeling is that the weakest link in our supply chain comes from something that Philips ultimately, and ironically, controls... the factory. Because Philips bought their share of the Healthcare market through M&A activity, they were left with factories very different types of cultures. Philips has allowed these different groups to keep their culture for the most part. These different factories do not communicate effectively out of pride and not wanting to change their practices. They have different ways of ordering product, and different fulfillment patterns from each factory. Philips needs to unify, and standardize the factories more in order to make the most of their investment. Philips also needs to let the employees know what the Healthcare culture and strategy are. Is it still quality above all else, or is it cost? The supply chain team feels the push from both. If this is done properly, the decision tree can be utilized better with the decisions made.

CASE STUDY QUESTIONS
(Answers Provided by Healthcare Professionals)

Briefly describe how your group supports the overall firm's objectives.

We support the Philips Healthcare objectives by constantly driving improvement through its logistic supply chain. The units supplied in Healthcare are very large and take a lot of efforts to complete a successful delivery. MRI units have 15,000lbs magnets and 10,000lbs to the rest of the system. CV systems are between 10-15,000lbs. X-rays are the smallest. We try to enhance, modify and make all aspects within the supply chain as efficient as possible. Our goal is quality deliveries in every aspect.

What is the business strategy for the organization?

Philips was a more traditional consumer electronics/lighting company and decided to strategically enter the Healthcare systems hardware industry ('94-'95), buying small and large businesses alike to fill out their portfolio. Philips saw the Healthcare industry as a rising value, whereas consumer electronics was in decline in profitability. Healthcare soon became the #1 priority on the Philips radar, while using the Philips name electronics as it's publicity and advertising.

What is the organizational structure?

The NA offices reports to Philips HQ in the Netherlands, with a dotted line to the factory and Philips Management. There are different Philips Business Units in NA that contact us to establish delivery coordination.

What are the inputs and outputs of the operations?

Within Philips Healthcare, our inputs are setting guidelines for HC deliveries, and mapping out the supply path from factory to hospital. Our outputs consist of reviewing delivery issues with the forwarders and carriers, doing root cause analysis, and corrective action for problem deliveries. Several calls are established to make sure all groups are aligned for a perfect delivery. The outputs are the final delivery and installations.

What is the corporate culture (values, principles, etc.)?

In years past the corporate culture was always quality first, cost second. However, cost has become a much larger factor over the last 2 years, equaling quality in importance. Not sure what part the new universal healthcare reform in the US will play in Philips profitability and scope.

What are the issues/concerns in production as it relates to market and industry changes?

Hospital deliveries must be precise. They must be on time with the right people, with the right tools. Obviously, R&D must keep up with innovations throughout the market to keep Philips competitive. Some recent issues have arisen with customs and FDA as they have input stricter regulations and employed more people to oversee their implementation. Also, Ocean and air carriers have made changes to their services due to the poor economy, which effectively lengthened Philips shipping lead times.

Describe the production process in the creation of the organization's primary products or services. Provide the key decisions in the process.

Philips HC systems are general within hospital standards, adding many available options, so they become a "build-to-suit" type of factory operation with a basic platform. The order comes in from sales with lead times of 1 year to 1 month, depending on the complexity. A delivery date is agreed to with the customer, and plans the build from there. The factory can save money by using ocean freight, but many times will run over by days or weeks, and be forced to air freight. The factory ship date is the first significant date when shipping, thereby setting the mode of transport. The next significant date is the receipt at the dock or airport, customs clearance, and FDA clearance. The system is then ready to ship to the Philips moving team, and finally to the hospital site. Any hiccup along the chain can lead to expedite charges so every step is watched carefully. Constant dialogue is kept with the customer to make sure the delivery date is intact.

What are the performance measures for success?

We measure (at time of site delivery) what Philips calls the "Perfect Delivery." As previously stated, we need the CV, MRI, CT, Nuc Med, or X-ray system to deliver as scheduled, on time, with the proper moving crew, with the proper tools. Tools include forklifts, pallet jacks, cordless screwdrivers, floor protectant, among others. WE also measure the effectiveness of the factory, the ocean/air forwarder, the ocean/air carrier, as well as the "last mile provider" moving crew. Our goal for perfect deliveries is 95-98% "on-time," and damage measurements are taken for each, as well as more subjective surveys, particularly with the customers involved.

What are your recommendations to make the organization more efficient and effective operations in the future?

My feeling is that the weakest link in our supply chain comes from something that Philips ultimately, and ironically, controls... the factory. Because Philips bought their share of the Healthcare market, they were left with very different types of factories. You have international factories and domestic factories... You have a different way of ordering product... You have different fulfillment patterns from each factory. Philips needs to unify, and standardize the factories more in order to make the most of their investment. Philips also needs to let the employees know what the Philips HC culture and strategy are. Is it still quality above all else, or is it cost? It can cause confusion and nervous decisions when the employees aren't sure what the focus is.

References

Jacobs, Chase, Aquilano (2009) *Operations and Supply Management*; 12th Edition. Chapter 6-7. New York: McGraw-Hill

Philips Healthcare Website- **http://www.healthcare.philips.com/main/**

Interview with a member of Philips US Supply Chain Project Management team, Joe Pajcic, conducted on 9/3/2010. Mr. Pajcic has over 25 years with the company.

Consultant Report

REPORT ON STRATEGIC IMPLEMENTATION: SMALL BUSINESSES IN AN UNSTABLE GOVERNMENT ENVIRONMENT

Daryl D. Green, Strategic Consultant
Performance Management & Logistics Associates

May 2006

EXECUTIVE SUMMARY

The purpose of this study is to address how small businesses can improve their survival and success rate in the public sector with a strategic approach to their operations. Case examples of four companies involved in contracting with the Department of Energy are evaluated. Data collection is achieved through qualitative analysis. The study concludes that successful small businesses can improve their chances of developing, growing, and maintaining their presence in government contracting through a strategic approach to business thinking. The application of these conclusions could increase the survival rate of small businesses operating in an unstable public environment. Researchers and practitioners interested in small businesses in the public sector will find the postulated concepts intriguing and beneficial.

Many small businesses dream about getting a large contract with the federal government, feeling that their lives would be easier if they did. However, there have been numerous occasions where small businesses have gone out of business due to being overwhelmed by government contracts. Many organizations do not strategically think about the long-term ramifications of their contracts. Most novice entrepreneurs develop a basic plan to secure a government bid and jump at any government opportunity. This is not strategic planning. Strategic thinking relates to a process that involves recognizing and focusing on issues and events that are significant in decision-making. It requires more than just planning, because strategic thinkers understand the interconnection and systematic consequences of given situations.

As with most government agencies, the Department of Energy (DOE) is impacted by external forces that influence its budget and contracting levels. DOE's budget resembles a rollercoaster. Most small businesses cannot afford this financial joyride, however. The General Accounting Office (GAO) conducted a study of leading companies to determine how they successfully reengineered their processes. It was found that the top leaders applied a strategic approach to their businesses. When using this method, companies found that they could save millions of dollars and improve the quality of services. Likewise, small businesses should be able to duplicate the benefits of strategic thinking in their operations over time (See Figure 1).

The purpose of this study is to evaluate the organizational planning of several small businesses in the midst of government changes that impact their businesses. This investigation is achieved by conducting a qualitative analysis of four small businesses contracted to DOE, to determine the effectiveness of their strategies in a public sector environment. While these organizational leaders have varied backgrounds and have followed a distinct career path, they each have reached a high level of success in the business world due to their keen business thinking.

SBA Business Model

The federal government has tried to assist entrepreneurs by providing a working business model and giving them contracting opportunities. The Small Business Administration (SBA) manages two special business assistance programs for small businesses – the 8(a) Business Development Program and the Small Disadvantaged Business Certification Program. Participants can receive sole-source contracts worth up to $5 million. The overall goal of this program is to groom these small businesses so that they can compete in an open market. In 1998, more than 6,100 firms participated in such programs and were awarded with $6.4 billion in federal contracts. The requirements for enrolling in these programs are extensive. The following SBA elements are used to select a potential small business in the program: (a) technical and managerial experience, (b) operating history, (c) access of capital and credit, (d) financial status, (e) record of performance, and (f) obtainment of any requisite licenses. Despite this leg up, the reality still exists that many of these small businesses fail even with the traditional planning process, especially business planning.

Exhibit 1

Figure 1. Key Elements for a Strategic Approach for Small Business Companies

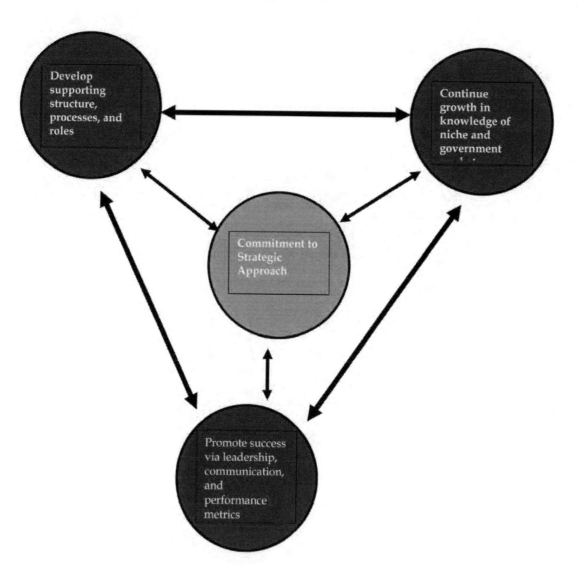

Land of Opportunity

Contracting with DOE can be very rewarding to small businesses. With an annual budget of about $23 billion, DOE is the largest civilian-contracting agency in the United States. Many small businesses are enchanted with DOE due to its attractive opportunities. To become a DOE contractor, the procurement office recommends the following for small businesses: (a) do the research, (b) prepare a company profile, (c) register the business in DOE's procurement system online, (d) develop a niche, (e) respond to DOE Sources Sought Notices, (f) match expertise with DOE bid, (g) be flexible, and (h) make the business customer-friendly. The federal government has a mandate that federal agencies award at least 23 percent of their contracts to small businesses. In 1994, DOE set a goal to have 25 percent of prime contracts go to small businesses; however, DOE awarded $3,029,100,000 in small contracts, or 34.5 percent.

DOE has a special office to assist small businesses with getting through the government front door. DOE purchases billions of dollars in goods and services, which include administrative services, facility management, construction, manufacturing, engineering, security, waste treatment, consulting, data processing, and a host of other organizational needs. There have been times when companies have secured these government contracts but did not have the resources to implement their plans. This study analyzes four small businesses at various maturity stages to gather information on how they are able to implement their plans. Visionary Solutions, LLC, LeGacy-Critique, Comfort Industries, Inc., and HME, Inc. are the small businesses interviewed; these companies have been able to survive the turbulent times in the public sector.

Preparation for Success

Small businesses must prepare their infrastructure to compete for government contracts. Cavanaugh Mims, the founder and CEO of Visionary Solutions, LLC, started his company with plenty of vision and energy but lacked the large brand name of his competitors. Mims started his company in 2000. Prior to that, he was an emerging DOE manager. A nuclear engineer by degree, he had twelve years managing government contracts, including four years managing a commercial power plant. He had spent several years managing environmental projects that provided him with an understanding of a potential niche in DOE. Mims explains, "I noticed that there were few minorities in field services. From my past [DOE] experience, I knew that this was an underserved area, and there was going to be a demand."

Armed with this knowledge, Mims started to lay the groundwork for his current organization. He started with one employee, himself. Currently, Visionary Solutions, LLC (VS) is a diverse minority-owned environmental management company, providing comprehensive services in transportation, training and technical assistance pertaining to hazardous waste and material disposition. VS clients include DOE, Department of Homeland Security, Nuclear Regulatory Commission, Department of Defense, and Tennessee Valley Authority, to name a few. Although VS has managed to secure private contracts, 90 percent of its work remains in the government sector.

James Smith, president and founder of Comfort Industries, Inc., developed his business from his previous experience and from the hard-knock school of business. Smith left the comfort of his secure job with a DOE contractor to pursue his own business venture in 1996. He explains that his family and personal attorney gathered to discuss the planning for his business. He started with a small janitorial service that many believed would fail. However, Smith continued to work his plan. Comfort Industries, Inc. is now a commercial and industrial service-contracting firm, providing concrete, rebar, framing, carpentry, project management, and construction cleaning services to government and private industry. Comfort Industries is a minority-owned small business with ten years of service.

DOE recently awarded a $27 million contract to LeGacy-Critique Joint Venture for administrative support services for the Oak Ridge Office in 2005. The contract employs 94 people. LeGacy is a woman-owned small business located in Brentwood, Tennessee. The president is Chiquita Young, an ex-DOE employee. Services to DOE include the following: reproduction, graphics, database management, technical writing and editing, photographic support, mail and file services, payment processing, visitor assistance, records retirement, security clearance, clearance processing, coordination of foreign national visits, and other general office duties. Critique had the DOE contract for administration for several years; however, its success elevated them from the 8(a) status so that they could not compete on this contract. Critique already had the staff, project experience, and customer relationships. Partnering with LeGacy became a logical strategy for Critique.

Frank Gethers, the project manager for this joint venture, views his management role as an integrator for employees as well as clients. With over 32 years of management experience in the DOE industry, Gethers understands the nature of contractor performance. Gethers explains, "Ninety-five percent of small businesses fail because they don't have a strategy or a business development [initiative]. You got to stay competitive." Gethers mentions that Critique had an outstanding rating with the government. Critique's success had elevated it out of the small business program. Matching up with an emerging small business, LeGacy was a perfect option for the Louisiana-based company. Gethers manages approximately 105 employees on this contract.

In September of 1996, HME, Inc. started up with a goal to pursue DOE work. Henry Perry, owner of the company, built his experience base in the DOE system and developed strategic relationships over the years so that he would be prepared once his opportunity arrived. Perry's experiences include over twenty years of construction experience, five years as a small business owner, and four years of management training. Perry worked for several companies gaining the experience he felt he needed to compete. Perry explains, "I had to go the contract route [working for someone else]. I didn't see getting into debt. Partnering is a winning situation." The mission of HME, Inc. is to provide customers with superior, reliable, and efficient management and construction services in a manner that supports total quality controls. Perry notes, "Dealing in the government arena forces you to think strategically." He got his real opportunity in 1999 on a government contract. However, he didn't have any workers to perform the work. Using a creative method and a persistent attitude, Perry was able to acquire these employees and perform the work. One success built on another. As a result, Perry found himself in demand.

From Vision to Implementation

Implementing a contract within the government is where strategy meets the reality test. How critical is it to implement a strategy while building and sustaining a competitive edge? Pat Summit, University of Tennessee coach and the "winningest" coach in NCAA history, argues, "Corporations have all kinds of competitors. You win with people." Leaders must engage their employees so that all components of the social technical system are in perfect alignment. Successful businesses are also able to operate in the present while preparing for the future. Organizational strategists call this duality. Mims kept his strategic thinking simple. Mims acknowledges that he used a supply chain approach for his customers. His success in the government-contracting arena has brought him closer to his vision. Mims strategically pointed at two key dates (2005 and 2010) toward which his organization has needed to build its infrastructure. These dates represent large DOE contracts paying big dividends.

From the very beginning, Mims relied on strategic alliances to build his organization. The first effort of his firm involved waste management and transportation. To secure his first contract, he had to depend on another company for trucks and drivers. He succeeded and continues to use strategic partnerships and contracts to build infrastructure toward the next key date. Although VS would be better positioned to secure small business contracts, Mims maintains that most of his contracts have been awarded in fully open competition. He notes that he has been able to beat larger competitors because his company has leveraged its strengths (being small, flexible, and innovative). Mims acknowledges, "We can make a decision in 30 seconds. Larger companies have to wait and talk it over with the board to see if it's a risk they are willing to accept. We are fast and flexible."

Likewise, Perry has built HME, Inc. slowly by adding additional skills mixes to his core capacities. He understands where he wants his company to be but explains it is a difficult task to reinforce this vision to staff. Perry clarifies, "No one is going to care about your business like you." Perry's hands-on approach promotes his vision and strategy to staff. However, he prefers to manage his managers. He provides guidance to his managers on what needs to be done. Perry set the standards by conveying the thought that "can't" is not in his company's dictionary. Perry provides the resources to meet his clients' needs and expects these needs to be met. He rewards good performance but finds no room for non-performance.

Smith has successfully managed to implement his plans for the company. His company moved beyond his initial step of janitorial services into other areas such as construction and project management. At one time, Smith had employees in seven states. Currently, he employs approximately 40 people. Comfort Industries, Inc. is headquartered in Knoxville, Tennessee. Partnering with his competitors has not been a part of Smith's strategy. Smith explained that when his first got started he tried to team with a competitor. He felt that they were the most attractive two companies on the bidding list. Smith was surprised to find the competitor was awarded the job. He knew the winning contractor but was unaware that he had bid on the job. It is a lesson he will always remember. Smith motto is to "have lots of plans in case one of them doesn't work out." Therefore, Smith plays "what if" scenarios in the contracting arena. His company has been successful. Smith admits that keeping the company's vision in the minds of employees is a difficult task. Smith explains, "I do it by example. Don't let anyone outwork you." It is an expectation he communicates to his staff by example. Smith can be found cleaning floors or doing duties he could delegate to his employees. Smith feels being connected to the work and employees is an advantage.

Frank Gethers understands the nature of implementing a vision in the LeGacy-Critique Venture. Gethers started in the DOE fusion program, where he was responsible for turning scientific concepts into proven results. Although Gethers realizes that most of his employees understand DOE expectations, he finds it important to reemphasize the company's mission. Gethers explains, "I believe in leadership. I try to conduct training for my managers to help them." He further explains that his organization uses several other techniques to keep this socio-technical system in harmony. LeGacy-Critiques' strategy includes management meetings and management retreats, quarterly meetings with all employees, and communication regularly with emails. Like other small businesses in this study, Gethers' company has had to turn down alliances and contracting because it was not in their long-term interest to pursue it. Gethers argues, "Why waste your time in an area that is not your niche?" Again, the myth that small businesses will accept any contract is not indicative of these successful small businesses.

Rocky Road

Past success for small businesses is no prerequisite for future success, especially in the governmental arena. Political and legal threats continue over SBA's role in providing small businesses with an economic advantage. Small businesses that were successful in one timeframe are not guaranteed to be successful in the next. Therefore, the past both helps and haunts a small business leader. It helps leaders because it gives them a reference point for solving similar problems. Therefore, it provides a leader with an arsenal of proven solutions. This strategy works in a stable, predictable environment. Conversely, it also betrays when this isn't the case. In times of rapid change and uncertainty, a leader's past knowledge becomes a liability because a leader can make the wrong assumptions. With the passing of time, many businesses undergo various stages in the life cycle of a business. Small businesses are not the exception but follow this business life cycle.

SBA notes numerous reasons why most small businesses fail, such as lack of experience, insufficient capital, and unexpected growth; however, market uncertainty can be one of the hardest things that small businesses must face. This problem can leave a small business owner in a quagmire of constant environmental change. The DOE market has changed. DOE has fallen short of its small business prime contracting objectives in four of the last five years. In 2005, DOE set a contracting goal for small businesses at 5.5 percent but fell short with only 4.15 awarded to small businesses. Therefore, the

DOE contracting pie is getting smaller while competition is increasing for small businesses. Shrinking government dollars is a concern for any business owner who wants to survive in the public sector. The four companies evaluated are now confronted with new challenges, which will test their business IQ (see Table 1).

Table 1. A Comparison of the Small Business Companies

	Comfort Industries	HME, Inc	LeGacy-Critique	Visionary Solution, LLC
Date Started	1996	September 1999	November 2005	Partnering 2000
Core Capabilities	Concrete Construction Framing/ Carpentry Rebar Construction	Facilities Support Management Services General Construction/Mowing Service Seismic Rehabilitation	Records Management Security Financial Support Administrative Support	Transportation and Logistics Training Technical Services and Waste Management Services
Target Market	Private	Government	Government	Government
Strategic Approach	"What-if" Scenarios Vision & Objectives Mega, Macro, & Micro Planning Paradigm Changers	Strategic Alliances Vision & Objectives Mega, Macro, & Micro Planning Paradigm Changers	Strategic Alliances Strategic Planning Paradigm Changers	Strategic Alliances Strategic Planning Vision & Objectives Mega, Macro, & Micro Planning Paradigm Changers
Future Outlook	Pursuit of Government Contracts, primarily DOE in 2006	Aggressive move on work outside of DOE for diversification in 2006	Current contract ends October 15, 2010	Secure two DOE Contracts (2006 & 2010) Diversify business mix in 18 months

Note: These approaches were gleaned through the discussions, interviews, and company literature. This table does not represent an exhaustive list of techniques used by these companies.

Visionary Solution, LLC has aggressively moved toward its major organizational milestones. Now awaiting the results of the first strategic milestone, Mims recognizes he will need to make some small adjustments to his plans. Although DOE continues to delay his strategic dates, Mims managed to exceed his expectations both of the number of employees he would need and of his financial backing. As VS continues to grow in size and location, Mims recognizes the potential problems. Mims explains, "The bigger you get, the harder it is to communicate." He acknowledges VS may not to use other communication tools to stay connected. His simple strategy, consisting of people, capital, opportunity/experience, and infrastructure, has allowed him to maintain steady growth and increase his core capacity. However, his competitors have not underestimated Mims, because more and more businesses are entering this once underserved market. Mims maintains he will not change his approach. He explains, "I don't change my plays. I just keep working to my strengths." Currently, VS is 95 percent DOE work and 5 percent non-DOE work. Mims' goal is to be at a 70-30 split in 18 months. Mims, however, admits he must adjust his planning to counter the government's uncertainty. Mims already acknowledges DOE will probably push back his second key dates several years.

Comfortable Industries, Inc. is seeking to expand in the government sector. Even with his government background as a contractor, Smith realizes that breaking into government contracting is no easy road. In the past, Smith has avoided strategic alignment with other companies. It is unclear if he will need to do so, however, in order to secure a viable contract. The first step for Smith has been getting his company DOE approval for a security clearance. Smith hopes that his prior experience in the DOE environment will be an asset for success in the DOE environment. Smith understands the challenges ahead. Smith explains, "I thrive on people telling me it can't be done."

Legacy-Critique has a history of success in the DOE system, but its future may still not be certain. Legacy-Critique's contract will run through 2010, with a 2-year base and three 1-year options. How will Legacy-Critique position itself at the contract closure? It is a thought that does not leave Gethers as he handles the day-to-day operations. Gethers maintains, "Copper and relationships are all we have. When I talk about copper, I'm talking about the metal that coins are made from. We can't lose focus of our customer. We need to watch the customer strategy." Gethers warns that his organization cannot be comfortable with its high ratings from the customer or in being the largest administrative contractor for DOE in Oak Ridge. Gethers acknowledges, "You need to stay competitive."

Perry can now focus on more out-year planning. His company is relatively stable. Since he and his wife are the senior leaders for the company, Perry considers the reality of retirement as he constructs for his company. Currently, his company is 98-percent financed through government contracts, primarily DOE. Perry focuses on more diversification (at least with the government) by partnering with another firm to secure another bid. Perry relates to struggle to get the right people for his niche business. For example, he explains it took him over five years to find the right accountant. In times past, he used accountants who were highly respected in their industry. Things would work well for a short period; however, there would be problems. Perry found that these accountants did not know how accounting works in a government environment.

It was a painful lesson for Perry. Now as he pursues a more diverse work portfolio, he will need to find the right work, the employees with the right skill mix, and the right strategic approach. He plans to work with another firm to pursue work with the Department of Defense. Perry understands the risks associated with doing this activity. He explains, "You have the cost of putting together a proposal and the issues associated with dealing with the whole procurement process." Obviously, managing a small business will continue to provide difficult challenges to these visionary leaders in the government environment.

The Future Ahead

The investigation critically evaluates four small businesses in the confines of a hostile business environment in the public sector. Leaders must interpret the organization's vision and communicate this vision to employees. There is a widely believed myth that 9 out of 10 new businesses fail in the first year. Headd conducted a study for SBA providing that this is not the case. He found that only one-third of new businesses closed under negative circumstances. However, Headd found the leading factors for business survival were good starting capital, an educated owner, adequate resources, and good people. In addition, this evaluation also demonstrated that successful small businesses could utilize strategic thinking in the public sector. These small businesses have looked beyond the present government contract to address future opportunities and challenges.

The cases that the present paper examines support the conclusion that successful small businesses can improve their chances of developing, growing, and maintaining their presence in government contracting with a strategic approach to business thinking. Applying this conclusion could increase the survival rate of small businesses operating in an unstable public arena. Researchers and practitioners interested in small businesses in the public sector will find the postulated concepts beneficial and significant because they widen contemporary assumptions about strategy thinking for small businesses engaged in government contracting.

Biographical Sketches

Daryl D. Green is a Department of Energy program manager with over 15 years of professional management experience. Mr. Green received a B.S. in Mechanical Engineering and an M.A. in Organizational Management. Currently, he is a Regent University Doctoral Candidate.

Endnotes

Mitchell, R. (2005). Strategic Thinking. Received on June 6, 2006 from http://www.csun.edu/~hfmgt001/st-thinking.htm.

General Accounting Office (2002). Best Practices: Taking a Strategic Approach Could Improve DOD's Acquisition of Services. Report to the Chairman and Ranking Minority Member, Subcommittee on Readiness and Management Support, Committee on Armed Services, U.S. Senate.

Small Business Administration (2006). 8(a) Business Development. Received on June 6, 2006 from http://www.sba.gov/8abd/indexprograms.html.

Department of Energy (2003). The Department of Energy Strategic Plan, 1-35.

Small Business Administration (2006). A Brave New World in Federal Procurement. SBA Success Magazine. Received on June 6, 2006 from http://www.sba.gov/library/successXV/16sbagovtprocuredoedoeversion.htm

Senate Report (2000). Small Business Federal Contract Set-Asides. Received on June 6, 2006 from http://thomas.loc.gov/cgi-bin/cpquery/?&dbname=cp105&sid=cp105G5jeT&refer=&r_n=sr

Department of Energy (2005). Small Business Receives Administrative Support Contractor for DOE's Oak Ridge Office. Received on June 12, 2006 from http://www.oro.doe.gov/media_releases/2005/r-05-039.htm.

Wacker, W., Taylor, J., & Means, H. (2000). The Visionary's Handbook. New York: HarperBusiness.

Small Business Administration (2006). Are You Ready? Received on June 6, 2006 from
http://www.sba.gov/starting_business/startup/areyouready.html

Butterfield, E. (2006). DOE Not Meeting Small Business Contracting Goals. Received on June 6, 2006 from
http://www.gcn.com/online/vo11_no1/40373-1.html.

Headd, B. (2003). Redefining Business Success: Distinguishing Between Closure and Failure, Small Business Economics, 21, 51-61.

Editorial/Commentary

HEADLINES: Father's Day Marks Untapped Male Feelings

Follow my lead. Here's the story. Tray is a hero among his peers. Tray has fathered several children from different women at his high school. Instead of his behavior repelling other young ladies, Tray finds himself a babe magnet. Tray sees himself as a "real man." While students see Tray as an American icon, adults see Tray's attitude as both arrogant and embarrassing. Tray's mother complains he's like his daddy – useless. Unfortunately, many people argue about the relevancy of fathers in the family structure. As millions celebrate Father's Day, we should reflect how effective fathers build a lasting legacy.

First, many critics argue the significance of men in today's family structure. According to the 2005 Census Report, there are 66.3 million fathers in the United States. There are 26.5 million fathers in a traditional family environment. There are 2.3 million single fathers living with children under 18 years old, up from 393,000 in 1970. There are also approximately 98,000 stay-at-home dads in America. Unfortunately, everything is not a pleasant story. There are 4.6 million fathers who pay child support, representing 84 percent of child support providers.

Fathers in traditional families are more involved than several decades ago. According to some studies, members of Generation X and Y are more likely to be family-focused. For example, Generation X fathers spent more time with children compared to Baby Boomer fathers. The impacts of the male influence in families may not be obvious. Does it really matter if a male is not a part of a child's life? Many people grew up with fathers whose primary role was as provider. The presence of a male figure in the home does impact children. Nationally syndicated columnist Leonard Pitts, Jr. wrote a book, Becoming Dad, where he surveys his tortured relationship with his abusive father. Pitts discusses how it affected his relationship with his own sons and daughters. He writes, "My father made our lives hell. And yet, for all of that, he was one thing many other fathers were not: He was there." Obviously, fathers are imperfect and this has been amplified in our society. Personally, I blame postmodern culture for fueling this negativism. Clearly, we are being bombarded with negative concepts of fathers. We do not live in an era of 'Leave It to Beaver' where dad knows best, and we have a caricature of Superman. My experience is that many fathers of our era are trying to do the right things; however, this gets lost in the day-to-day drama of life. Fathers are necessary to achieve a healthy family balance even though they are not celebrated as such. Obviously, there are numerous examples of deadbeat dads, abusers, and downright losers. But, if society buys into the notion that fathers are useless, how do we give our children a sense of hope for the future? We must showcase the positive things fathers are doing in the community while counseling the misguided ones. America cannot survive without real fathers and real men.

About Daryl Green:

Daryl Green, author of *Awakening the Talents Within*, mentors young men across the country. He is a national columnist and residents in Knoxville with his family. For more information, you can contact him at info@darylandestraletta.com.

Published in the Knoxville News Sentinel

Employment Letter (pitch)

PMLA

PMLA

P. O. Box 32733 ~ Knoxville, TN 37931 ~ USA

Phone (865) 602-7702 ~ Fax (865) 602-7702

pmla@att.net

September 10, 2012

Dr. Kate Atchley, Department Head
University of Tennessee
Department of Management
408 Stokely Management Center
Knoxville, TN 37996-05345

Dear Dr. Atchley:

Subject: Adjunct Letter of Interest

The purpose of this letter is to convey my interest in teaching at your university in the Fall of 2007 and to enquire about the opportunities that you have available as an adjunct professor. I have a deep passion for teaching and love working with young people. I have both practical experience in managing multiple million dollar projects as well as experience with teaching at an academic institution.

Currently, I work for the Department of Energy as a program manager with over 17 years of management experience. My background includes project management, research and development, technology development, technology transfer, waste management, robotics, characterization, and a deactivation & decommission project. My wife and I also own a consulting business. We have extensive experience with making management decisions in public, private, and non-profit organizations.

I received a BS in mechanical engineering and an MA in Organizational Management, and am currently a doctoral candidate in strategic leadership at the Regent University School of Leadership Studies. I have also written several books and have published over 100 articles in the field of decision-making and leadership. I believe that my management experiences and my education have given me a unique perspective in understanding emerging trends.

For the last several semesters, I have taught a variety of courses at Knoxville College as a visiting professor for DOE. I have also served as a visiting professor or adjunct professor to several schools including Pellissippi State Technical Community College, Johnson C. State University, and Knoxville College. I have first-hand experience with youth-oriented problems, and working with community, church, and other organizations. As a result, I use interactive teaching techniques to engage my students.

Attached is my academic vita for your review. Please let me know if there is any position available for management/business areas for your department and if you feel I am a match, by March 30, 2007. Please feel free to call me at (865) 241-6198. Thanks in advance for your consideration.

Respectfully,

Daryl Green

Guest-Blogger Article

Guest-Blogger: "Is Real World Application for Real?" – Noriko Chapman

Some MBA students find there is no relevancy in what they learn in class and the practical world. Yes, I was one of these doubters until I was engaged by one of my professors in an operations management course at Lincoln Memorial University. The end result was assisting a local non-profit organization, writing my first book, and being thrust upon the expert stage. Operations management (OM) should be important to non-profit organizations too. With shrinking funds for programs and a more competitive environment, non-profit organizations will need to rethink their corporate strategies for future success.

This reality means managing their operations more efficiently and shifting their traditional thinking to a more entrepreneurial approach. Unlike businesses that are driven primarily by profit, nonprofits use any monies earned to be put back into the organization to cover their own expenses, operations, and programs. In 2005, there will be approximately 1.4 million non-profit organizations registered to the IRS according to "Non-Profit Market" by Closerware.com.

My OM project called a "Real World Application" project was on the Tennessee Vocational Rehabilitation based in Maryville, Tennessee; it is one of these non-profit organizations looking for more operational effectiveness in the future.

Tennessee Vocational Rehabilitation is a federal and state-funded program run by the Tennessee Department of Human Services Division of Rehabilitation Services to assist individuals of work age with physical and/or mental disabilities to compete successfully with others in earning a livelihood.

Based on the research data from the 2007 American Community Survey, approximately 12.8% of Americans between the ages of 21 and 64 have a disability. In Fiscal Year 2009, the Division of Rehabilitation Services provided services to 30,289 individuals in Tennessee and 27,932 individuals met the eligibility criteria of the program.

It is projected that 30,000 individuals will receive services and that 27,000 individuals will meet the eligibility criteria of the program and receive services during Fiscal Year 2011. Tennessee Vocational Rehabilitation in Maryville supplies automotive parts to Denso where I work.

The work usually requires a packaging or simple sub-assembly task while is a training tool for clients to learn work skills and experience. The average training length is 4 months. However, I found all the staff being occupied with the daily routine and the primary mission of serving the clients. The staff didn't have enough time to observe and evaluate its capacity and capability.

Also, the center manager was afraid of committing to additional work and contracts due to the unique labor population and the number of fluctuating clients. My recommendations were to provide a tool to analyze the capacity frequently and to establish the fine balance of time-sensitive and non time-sensitive jobs to absorb the fluctuations. For instance, the center can prioritize and focus on the time-sensitive jobs for the Just-in-time customer due to high absenteeism.

Working with Dr. Green, I published my results. My new book, Second Chance, provides non-profit organizations with information about how to useoperations management tools to make them more efficient and better equipped to assist their clients and constituents in meeting their needs.

Nonprofit organizations like for profit organizations must find innovative ways to compete with others. This includes competing on several dimensions which are (a) cost or price, (b) quality, (c) speed, (d) delivery reliability, and (e) coping with change. The concepts, theories, tools, technology or reading materials learned in the classroom are not to keep in a closet.

They are to practice in a real world for an advanced career or a way to help organizations who need the knowledge and expertise. The support can be a time study, data analysis, plotting graphs for visual control, standardized work, material flows, and finally mock interviews for clients who were ready for job placement.

I just had to ask the very last question to a client during a mock interview at the center. "How did you know about this center? How did the experience at the center help you prepare for a job?" He answered without any hesitation, "It's the best thing ever happened to me. I get up every morning and cannot wait to come here. The experience gave me skills and confidence to find a real job. " He also appreciated his mother for finding out the program and encouraging him to pursue.

There are many other individuals with disabilities who can benefit from the service like the client who I interviewed. How can we optimize the capacity to accommodate more clients without increasing the operation costs? I learned that I can make a difference, using my operational experience.

As a surprising result, I found a practical side of my MBA learning by helping others in the community. If we spend approx. 40 hours per week for a careerjob, 2~3 hours a week of investment outside of the work seems to be very little. However, you will be amazed by the positive impact you can make for the people who need help.

Don't underestimate your talent! It can be fully utilized and appreciated outside of the classroom. Pursuing a degree is an accomplishment, but we can even capitalize the talent and skills even further by reaching out. It's a genuine accomplishment.

Please comment on Ms. Chapman's points.

© 2011 by Noriko Chapman

Noriko Chapman helps social causes as an industry expert.

Noriko Chapman is the mother of two children. She lives in Maryville, Tennessee. She is a Production Control supervisor in the Instrument Cluster Division of DENSO Manufacturing Tennessee, Inc. She worked at DENSO specializing in production planning, new products start up, service parts operations, supply chain and warehouse operations for 16 years and for 2 years as a full- or part-time translator at the beginning before the first Tennessee DENSO plant was built. Given the fact that she was raised in Japan, she wrote a chapter "Japanese Practices in an Autoparts Plant" for the book, EFFECTS OF JAPANESE INVESTMENT IN A SMALL AMERICAN COMMUNITY by Scott Brunger and Young-Bae Kim. Her Maryville College undergraduate research paper, "A Dramaturgical Analysis of Japanese Organization Behavior," won an undergraduate award by North Central Sociological Association. She is currently attending Lincoln Memorial University MBA program and now serves on the board of directors for the Tennessee Department of Human Services, Division of Rehabilitation Services.

Published on Nuleadership Revolution Blog

How-To/Instructional Column

Building Good Father-Daughter Relationships

INTRODUCTION

In 1985, The *Color Purple* made its debut into America's culture. The story follows the life of Celie, a young black girl growing up in the South. At 14 years old, she becomes pregnant by her stepfather. During her journey through adulthood, Celie would face a difficult life. She was riddled with doubt, low self-esteem, and lacked any meaningful relationships with men. Her misery could be traced back to the dysfunctional relationship with her stepfather. Media outlets bombard society with themes of irresponsible and abusive fathers in the home. These men lack any emotional courage to deal with their daughters. Therefore, the emotional connection is passed to mothers. In our society, young ladies face tremendous cultural pressures. Everyone wants to fit in. However, some girls pursue it at any cost. Looking for love in all the wrong places often leads them down a path of destruction. For example, America has the highest rates of teen pregnancy in the western industrialized world. According to one estimate, one in eight teens suffer from depression. Some problems can be traced back to the lack of father-daughter relationships. The US Department of Health and Human Services report that 63% of youth suicides are from fatherless homes.

THE FACTS

A good father-daughter relationship can make a difference. A number of significant studies demonstrate that high levels of involvement by fathers contribute to children's wellbeing. Noted sociologist Dr. David Popenoe argues, "Involved fathers bring positive benefits to their children that no other person is likely to bring." According to the Annie E. Casey Foundation, the number of teen mothers in the United States is on the decline. Some people would profess it is due to better education. Dr. Bruce Ellis, a psychology professor at the University of Canterbury in Christchurch, explores the significance of fathers in a daughter's life: "It is also likely that girls who have high-investing fathers in the home tend to begin sex and dating at a later age and thus have less pheromone exposure to male dating partners in early adolescence."

CONCLUSION

Contrary to popular belief, I see many men who are trying to teach their daughters to carry themselves with dignity. I hear them tell their daughters "you can be anything that you want to be." Some tell their daughters to pick their friends and relationships wisely: "If you lie down with dogs, you will get fleas." Therefore, the positive messages of good father-daughters relationships are lost on foolishness and sensational journalism. The real fathers just continue to instruct their daughters and set proper examples for them. There were plenty of men carrying themselves respectfully and being an example to the young men who would escort their daughters. Dedicated fathers will do anything to help their daughters be successful. In the Color Purple, Celie was denied a good father-daughter relationship. We can only hope that today's fathers will not miss out on this opportunity with their own daughters. Let's pray that it is not too late.

Daryl D. Green writes on contemporary issues impacting emerging leaders in a variety of sectors (businesses, societies, global communities, etc). He has over 20 years of assisting organizations.

Published by Knoxville News Sentinel

Interviews

Women's History Month in East Tennessee

By Dr. Daryl D. Green

Women are flexing their muscles in East Tennessee. Media darlings such as Dolly Parton highlight the power of women in their profession. According to Fortune Magazine, 15 Fortune 500 Companies are run by women. On the government front, leading the charge are Secretary of State Hillary Clinton and House Speaker Nancy Pelosi. Yet, many people forget the impacts that career success has on professional women.

This article focuses on the issues facing professional women in the area. Liza Fuller is a government program manager with a decade of experience in handling difficult environmental issues in East Tennessee. Her real name is not disclosed to protect her since she works in a small industry. She is a midlife professional, married with two children. She is highly educated with a degree from Vanderbilt University and also an advanced degree. She exists in a mostly male dominated industry. She assisted her organization with celebrating Women History Month. In truth, Fuller is a genuine role model for today's working professional.

Discuss your heroes when you were growing up, and how they have shaped you as a person.

I have always spent a lot of time around adults with PhDs so I have not really been much of a kid. My heroes were astronauts, teachers, John Kennedy, my parents, and strangely enough Vanderbilt basketball players, probably because my dad took me to the games. I really admired Tommy Arnholt, a very good, but not very tall, basketball player in the early 1970s, and admired him more when I found out he also helped with the Special Olympics. My dad also took me to college archaeology lectures and started my love for discovery, adventure and science. My mom and dad also taught me to love the earth and take care of it.

Describe what most people say are your best qualities.

My nickname was "United Nations" because I could talk to anybody about anything and I have great diplomacy skills. I am also very helpful and kind. I am the kind of person who likes to please people.

Discuss your professional career and education (your progression as a professional woman).

I got my B.S. at age 20 and my M.S. at age 41. If I had time I think, I would to go back to school and focus on epidemiology and try to figure out what we are doing to cause so many cases of cancer and other problems and what part of our modern life should be changed to attain better health for all people. I think I would have been a great detective in another life.

217

What are the challenges facing working women in the workforce today?

Women are still expected to work harder than men to prove themselves and avoid criticism. Attractive women still get grief about being promoted for reasons other than their own merit and it's not fair. The other challenge is trying to make a fair amount of time for your kids while they are young and balancing their needs with those needs of a demanding boss or demanding job.

What are issues associated in a relationship where a female makes more than her husband? Do roles change?

In my case my husband is unemployed. Yes, I ask him to do more housework and to cook and he takes the primary role with the kids. Are more demands made on the female? Yes. I still have to do the housework but I get lots of help. You have to have a strong partnership and accept all the help your partner gives and not dwell on the money. You also have to be financially disciplined and teach your kids to be also.

Do you feel it is possible to climb the corporate ladder as a female without sacrificing your family?

No, there is always a sacrifice because you spend more time away from your family. Is the issue the same for males having the same advantages in today's modern society? Yes, I think so, but they usually have wives who take care of the home and kids for them.

What tips would you give to young professional women (Generation Y) coming into corporate America so that they can progress successfully?

You know what, I have no idea what their expectations are. Give your best to your job while you are there. Just remember that your family will be there to love you when you get a bad review or have a fight with your boss, so always put them first. Work at home after the kids go to bed, if you have to, and tell your kids and husband every day that you love them.

© 2010 by Daryl D. Green

Published at Knoxville Examiner

Letter to the Editor

National Library Week:

A Salute to America's Library Institution

Many people will miss the importance of this week in changing people's lives. It is National Library Week, April 2-8th. The library serves as a catalyst in equipping students in developing future leaders for a changing world. There are 120,000 libraries in the US, including public libraries (about 8,900 systems with almost 16,000 separate locations), school libraries (almost 100,000), academic libraries (over 3,000), and specialized libraries for corporate, legal, medical, and religious institutions (over 10,000)

As taxpayers demand individual pay more for social resources provided by governments, many pragmatists argue the merits of expanding library resources. Fortunately, this national week honors the contributions of libraries in connecting our communities to books and other learning materials. America's owes a debt of thanks to the public libraries. It is a part of American history and a rich source of information. Many people have gone from rags to riches while reading books. Many of the great icons in history such as Abraham Lincoln and Martin Luther King, Jr. had a passion for reading.

I have learned to appreciate the many resources available in these institutions. I have spent many hours in libraries across the country, conducting extensive research for clients and completing personal projects. The libraries represent an invisible treasure to many. Please don't take them for granted. Americans can continue to teach their children to dream big dreams. Books can be a tool to make dreams become a reality. Visit a library this week and say thanks to your local library staff.

Daryl Green, Author of Awakening the Talents Within

Published in USA Today

Magazine Article

Getting the Obama Daughters Ready for School: Seven Preparation Tips for Parents

Karen works hard to make ends meet as a divorcee with five kids. She loves her summers because they are less hectic. During the school year, Karen fights a torturing schedule of kids' activities. Tomorrow will start another school year. Karen wonders how her life will change.

Introduction

Summer is almost over. It's time to refocus your child's summer schedule to the rigidness of reading, writing, and arithmetic. Even the President's children are no exception to this reality. With an economic downturn dampening their summer, many parents are having a difficult time directing their full attention to their child's preparation for the new school year. Yet, many experts contribute a child's success in life to the influences of their parents. Therefore, it is important that parents carefully consider their planning for the year. This article provides insight for overcoming the stresses of managing a hectic school life for working parents.

Obama's Summer Lesson

The Obama daughters' summer provided better preparation for the school year. However, this was not due to chance. Sasha and Malia Obama spent a wonderful summer filled with foreign travel, dignitaries, community service, celebrity engagements, and two months of a school-free existence. According to the New York Times newspaper, their summer travels included Moscow, Rome, and Ghana. In fact, the Obama parents viewed the kid's international experiences as a real-time history lesson. President Barack Obama noted "[his daughters] see the world and then report back to us on what they are seeing."

Additionally, the daughters participated in community service such as volunteering at Fort McNair (VA). Yet, even the family stationed at 1600 Pennsylvania Avenue could not escape the discipline of parenting. Michele Obama stated, "The television and the computers are off all day until after dinner and right before bed time." As summer fun fades, Sasha and Malia turned their attention to another year at Sidwell Friend School. Like so many other students, their success will be determined by the preparation of their parents for their education.

The School Preparation

Are parents prepared for this school year? Managing family time is an important part of preparation. Many people get overwhelmed with balancing work and family; they can obtain a big dose of "Back-to-School" Blues. According to a CareerBuilder.com survey, one-half of workers reported that they feel a great deal of job stress. Forty-four percent of working moms admitted being preoccupied with work while at home.

Today's children are so busy that they need their own blackberries to keep up with their schedules. Therefore, parents must exercise discretion in choosing their children's activities. Parent should make sure that children's activities enhance and stabilize family relationships. The following are helpful tips for parents with active children to ensure a successful school year:

1. Develop a strategy for dealing with family issues beforehand.
2. Prioritize the important things to your family.
3. Create goals to support your family objectives.
4. Establish a family calendar to better schedule events around your family.
5. Set aside time to listen to your children.
6. Share time with family by setting aside at least one day a week.
7. Limit your personal commitments.

Conclusion

Many parents view the school year as another exercise in patience. Without the proper guidance and direction, some children can have a disappointing school year. Like Sasha and Malia, children need parents to better prepare them for the rigors of school life. Parents can use this new school year to build better relationships. By adequately preparing activities and setting priorities, parents can minimize the pressures of a new school year. It is not too late to establish control.

About the Columnist:

Dr. Daryl D. Green writes on contemporary issues impacting individuals, businesses, and society across the globe. With over 18 years of management experience, Dr. Green's expertise has been noted and quoted by *USA Today, Ebony Magazine,* and *Associated Press*. For more information, you can go to **http://stores.lulu.com/darygre** or http://www.darylgreen.org.

Published in Black Pearl Magazine

Query Letter

September 10, 2012

Dr. Wade H. Shaw
Engineering Management Program
Florida Institute of Technology
150 West University Boulevard
Melbourne, FL 32901

Dear Dr. Shaw:

Subject: Leading Workers While Supporting Organizational Values

The purpose of this letter is to transmit my article to IEEE Engineering Management Review Magazine for your professional review. I am suggesting a 1,310-word article entitled "Leading a Socio-Technical System to Support Organizational Values" which provides an understanding on how to maximize the socio-technical system in an organization. The primary goal is to explore man-machine interface as it relates to organizational effectiveness. This insight gained through this research may lead to better management strategies for technical leaders.

Currently, I work for the Department of Energy as a program manager. I have spent over 15 years managing federal contracts. I have a BS in mechanical engineering and a MA in organizational management. I am currently pursuing a doctoral degree in leadership from Regent University. I have written over 100 commercial articles and presented several technical papers at various

conferences.

Attached is this article. I am very flexible to your suggestions. If you any questions please feel free to call me at (865) 241-6198. Thanks in advance for your consideration.

Respectfully,

Daryl Green

Appendix B

Book Publishing for Professionals

Today's professionals should consider creating a book with the end in mind. Entrepreneur publishing (EP) can provide this mechanism since it is outcome-driven, customer-focused, and information rich. If you are only interested in "you," then this is not the approach for you. Entrepreneurs focus on solving market problems; good results produce wealth, influence, and power. In this scenario, a writer clearly understands his or her audience and uses that information to achieve his or her personal objectives. You have done your homework. You write to address a problem or issue in the market, or for a certain audience. This process is not directly about you; it's about solving two problems at once: filling a market need and becoming successful in the process. Disseminating information and advice on a specific subject can elevate you to a new level in terms of influencing others. Entrepreneur publishing has the following characteristics: (a) it focuses on end results; (b) it seeks to solve a problem in society, business, or the general marketplace; (c) it aims for a target audience; (d) it applies marketing strategies; (e) it utilizes modern technology such as a print-on-demand strategy; and (f) it builds on the effective approach of self-publishing successes. To be successful, authors should target their message to a specific audience.

With the emerging publishing technology, the question no longer is, *"Can* you be published?" but, *"How* will you be published?" There are numerous options to choose from in your publishing venture. As we have seen, the major options include the traditional publisher, vanity press, small press, academic press, self-publishing, and publishing portal. Today's authors can develop critical information, determine how it is to be disseminated, and take it directly to their target audience. In fact, targeting involves identifying and focusing on a specific group that is most likely to purchase your book.[34]

---

[34] *Get Published* by Susan Driscoll & Diane Gedymin

Table 1. Comparison of Publishing Options

Publishing option	Characteristics	Advantage / Disadvantage
Major Publisher	• Publishes over 100 books a year • Seeks established writers or celebrities • Based on a business model (profit) • 20% of their books generate 80% of their profit • Prefers literary agent as writer contact • Established book distribution system	**Advantage** Better recognition & prestige More possibility of creating a bestseller Established relationships within book industry More promotional dollars for authors Larger ability for influencing target audience **Disadvantage** Prefers established authors or celebrities Publishing time extremely long (over 18 months) Prefers working with literary agent High price of literary agents – finding one & commission (about 15%) Little input or control for author on book Royalties between 5-15 % for midlist authors
Small Press	• Publishes less than 10 books a year • Usually publishes to a niche or specialty market • Will generally work with a writer directly	**Advantage** Focused and passionate about subject and author Targeted marketing strategy Some relationships within the publishing industry Royalties may be negotiable More input during the publishing process **Disadvantage** Not well recognized versus major publisher Limited budget for promotions May not be as well organized as major publisher

Vanity Press	• Bad reputation in book and publishing industry • Acceptance of all potential writers as possible cash stream • Sub-par quality and editing • Market through magazine ads and yellow pages (800 numbers)	**Advantage** Will accept most writers Easy access for potential writers **Disadvantage** Bad reputation in publishing community Associated with business scams Blackballed among retailers, book reviewers, and others in the book industry Make money primarily on selling to the author Known to take advantage of authors Low quality and editing
Academic Press	• Publishes less than 10 books a year • Usually publishes to a niche or specialty market • Will generally work with a writer directly • Limited budget and limited relationship with book distributors	**Advantage** Better recognition More prestige Established relationships within book industry More promotion dollars for authors **Disadvantage** Prefers established authors or celebrities Little input or control for author on book Royalties between 5-15 % for midlist authors Publishing time extremely long (over 18 months)
Self-Publishing	• Publishes less than 10 books a year • Usually publishes to a niche or specialty market	**Advantage** More control Bigger profit (0% - 100%) Speed & adaptability to market changes Ease to market to target or niche audience Apt to apply emerging technologies

	• The writer is the publisher • Limited budget and limited relationship with book distributors	**Disadvantage** Industry perception as 2nd tier writer Responsibility for all publishing aspects Increased necessity for marketing strategy Less-established or no distribution channel
Publishing Portals	• Print-on-demand technology • Will publish anyone, in general (similar to vanity press) • Most companies are Internet-based * Established distribution channel	**Advantage** More control Larger royalties than traditional (20% >) Speed & adaptability to market changes Ease to market to target or niche audience Apt to apply emerging technologies **Disadvantage** Minimal promotion Limited exposure in traditional bookstores Restrictive contracts Publishing industry view as negative Book reviews skeptical of POD books

Publishing portals are distinguished by their self-publishing characteristics, their similarity to the vanity press, and a heavy reliance on emerging technologies. Many provide one-stop shopping for all of your publishing needs (editing, printing, marketing, distribution, etc.). At the heart of this technology is print-on-demand (POD) technology. POD allows authors to print books one at a time or in smaller quantities than at a traditional press. It is a cost effective approach to testing a market and growing a base of followers. Like other self-publishing initiatives, POD companies make it difficult for books to get into traditional bookstores. Readers need to request the book before a bookstore will order it. However, this is actually an advantage for an entrepreneur who is creating demand.

There are also POD companies that only do printing and do not offer the full suite of services. However, we recommend that you go with an established POD company that has relationships with the book retailers and distributors, such as Book Surge (Amazon.com) or iUniverse.com (Barnes & Noble). With this approach, individuals can expect to get royalties between 20-50%; however, some such companies do not provide royalties at all. This is better than a traditional publisher but your profit is limited. Remember, most POD publishers make money from authors buying their own books. Most POD writers sell less than 200 books on average. Pay close attention to the contract. Make sure that you have an "out clause" with the POD company in case you are discovered by a major publisher or you are unhappy with this POD publisher. Consider other products such as e-books or hardback books. This can increase your product line with little effort.

Below are some top picks for this EP process:

Createspace (www.createspace.com) – publishing affiliation: Amazon.com

Xlibris (www.xlibris.com) – publishing affiliation: Random House

Morris Publishing (www.morrispublishing.com)

BookSurge (www.booksurge.com) – publishing affiliation: Amazon.com

Outskirtspress (www.outskirtspress.com)

Lulu (www.lulu.com)

iUniverse.com (www.iuniverse.com) – publishing affiliation: Barnes & Noble

Authorhouse (www.authorhouse.com)

Bookmasters (www.bookmasters.com)

Arbor Books (www.arborbooks.com)

Reduce your risk by doing your homework. All of these companies have great reputations. An individual should pick a POD company that meets their needs and provides a high level of service. Visit their websites. Compare your top three POD companies with each other. Compare each package. Analyze the cost, contracts, and publishing services. Contact some authors on their list (you can usually find an email on the Internet) to see if they are happy. Most will provide a candid evaluation. This is a good strategy. Most of the publishing submittal is online via email. It can work smoothly. I now enjoy it.

Appendix C

Tentative Publishing Schedule

Every writer should develop a unique marketing strategy for each book. Having a schedule is part of this process. Every person has a different method for launching his or her book. Below is a publishing schedule I like to use, which can serve as a general guide:

Major Publishing Actions	Estimated Timeframe
Develop an idea	varies
Research target audience	2-4 weeks
Review similar books in subject area	2 weeks
Write chapter outline for book and preface	1-2 weeks
Write a marketing strategy for book	1-2 weeks
Complete final book manuscript	2-12 months (based on complexity and schedule)
Obtain copyright	1-2 months

Prepare Book for Publication	1-2 Months
Professional editing	1-6 weeks
Bookcover design	3 weeks
Interior book design	3 weeks
Submit to printer (electronically or mail)	1-5 days
Printing	4-6 weeks
Launch promotional strategy	ASAP

Made in the USA
San Bernardino, CA
27 July 2017